Grace Moments

JULY–SEPTEMBER 2024

TIME OF GRACE®

Published by Straight Talk Books
P.O. Box 301, Milwaukee, WI 53201
800.661.3311 / timeofgrace.org

Printed in the United States of America
ISBN: 978-1-949488-93-7

JULY

You are a chosen people, a royal priesthood,
a holy nation, God's special possession, that you
may declare the praises of him who called you
out of darkness into his wonderful light.

1 PETER 2:9

Cross it out
Matt Ewart

I know someone who loves to make extra-spicy salsa. (It's someone at my church.) I also know someone who likes to eat extra-spicy salsa. (That's me.) We get along great.

One day as this person was giving me some jars of salsa, they shared other things too. Along with the jars of salsa, I was delighted to find some homemade jam.

But when I got home and looked at the jars of jam, I had to stop and laugh. This person had reused some jar lids that had previously been used for salsa. I could clearly see the words *HOT SALSA* crossed off with a marker and the words *BLUEBERRY JAM* written beneath them.

It made me laugh because I wish life worked like that. I wish I could just cross out the things I want to change and write something new. But I don't have a marker big enough for that. And even if I did, my attempt to relabel something wouldn't change what's beneath.

But the cross of Jesus is big enough to both relabel our circumstances and change what's beneath. Because death has been defeated, we can look at TRIALS and consider them PURE JOY.

And because of what Jesus did, my identity as SINNER has been changed to SAINT.

"But you were washed, you were sanctified, you were justified in the name of the Lord Jesus Christ and by the Spirit of our God" (1 Corinthians 6:11).

Challenge accepted
Liz Schroeder

My accountability partner recently gave me a challenge. The challenge was to start every one of my prayers with praise.

Why praise? Because starting with praise reframes all the other things I pray about: my worries, my shame, my petitions, and my gratitude.

While Paul was in prison(!), he issued a challenge to the church in Philippi: **"Rejoice in the Lord always,"** and then a little louder for those in the back, **"I will say it again: Rejoice!"** (Philippians 4:4).

I'm no Greek scholar, but I am a word nerd with an English degree and Google, so let me tell you what I found out about the word *rejoice*. It is in the present active imperative, second person plural, and means to be "favorably disposed to God's grace." In other words, "Y'all better rejoice and keep on rejoicing because you're going to see the grace of God everywhere you look."

I was skeptical that starting every prayer with praise would make a difference. I also worried that my needs wouldn't be met and that it would feel forced or inauthentic.

But I accepted the challenge. Even when my heart is heavy, I start with praise. It changes my focus from what I want changed in my life to the God who never changes. My gaze shifts from self to Savior, and I am beginning to see his grace in unexpected places.

Not to be dramatic, but it's changing everything. Are you up to the challenge?

Cast it away
Ann Jahns

I'm an expert worrier. I've had over 50 years to perfect my craft. One of the hardest verses in Scripture for me to live is 1 Peter 5:7: **"Cast all your anxiety on** [God] **because he cares for you."**

I started thinking about the word *cast* in that verse. In the original Greek, it's *epiripto*—a verb of forceful action. It's not a gentle handing off or setting aside. It's more of a hurling something away with purpose. Picture a weary cowboy heaving a weighty pack onto the broad back of his horse, which will now easily carry it for him. That horse was built to bear that burden.

God asks for our burdens. He wants the mess we throw his way because he loves us. He even invites it: **"Come to me, all you who are weary and burdened, and I will give you rest"** (Matthew 11:28).

Are you aching over a fallout with a loved one? Cast it on God. Are you battling a persistent sin? Cast it on God. Are you shattered from a diagnosis? Cast it on God. Cast it all onto him in prayer—from the smallest, nagging pebble of doubt to the largest, crushing boulder of fear.

I invite you to bring your worries to God right now: *Lord, today I cast _____ onto your powerful shoulders. I can't handle this on my own. I cast it onto you because I know that you love me, have a plan for me, and will give me the deep and abiding rest only you can give. Amen.*

Attitude of gratitude
Katrina Harrmann

Have you ever gotten a thank-you card? Doesn't it warm your heart and make you feel like the gift you gave was completely worth the expense?

Have you ever NOT gotten a thank-you for something you gave? Me too. If I'm being honest, it seriously made me rethink my generous gift!

Take a moment to read the story of Jesus healing ten lepers on the way to Jerusalem (Luke 17:11-19). There's a very important nugget in it. Out of the ten lepers, only one turned back (once he'd been healed) and thanked Jesus.

Jesus got one thank-you note out of ten. ONE. For a *life-changing* gift.

I believe this story teaches us that saying thank you— showing gratitude—is a *huge* part of the process when it comes to answered prayers.

Do you return to God when he answers your prayers and say thank you? Oof. I think we *all* tend to fall short, don't we? We often pray for days or weeks for something we really want. Then when we get it, we skip on our merry way without a backward glance at the healer.

Take time today to thank God for answered prayers. And as we celebrate Independence Day in the U.S., remember to pray for your country and its leaders. God answers those prayers too.

Just as you enjoy getting a well-deserved thank-you note, your heavenly Father loves to receive your gratitude and praise! And boy is he ever worthy of it!

"Give thanks to the Lord, for he is good; his love endures forever" (Psalm 107:1).

Look up to Jesus
Jon Enter

Do you have a family member or friend who messes up perpetually, who just can't get it together? You and I, on the other hand . . . puff out our chests a little bit . . . know better and live better, right?

But the person who goes to strip clubs, who clicks through porn, who cheats on their spouse, who's quick to lie, who drinks too much, who disrespects their parents, who despises another . . . that person is no different from you or me. You may or may not do something on that list, but if you don't, you have your own sinful vices.

Sinning less than other people won't get you to heaven. **"Therefore no one will be declared righteous in God's sight by the works of the law."** Following and trying to fulfill God's law can't save you. Being a better version of yourself won't save you. It's never enough. **"Rather, through the law we become conscious of our sin"** (Romans 3:20).

Don't look down on others because they sin differently from you. Look up to Jesus! Look up to the One who was placed on a cross to heal your very life. Look up to the One who knows just how hard life can be, just how difficult it is to get up each day to face new problems and new pains. Look up to the One who walked this earth out of love for his Father and for you—his purpose was to save you. Look up to Jesus!

Lying lips
Andrea Delwiche

"I call on the LORD in my distress, and he answers me. Save me, LORD, from lying lips and from deceitful tongues" (Psalm 120:1,2).

I read these words, and two applications come to mind.

The first is what seems to be most intended by the text. This psalmist asks the Lord to protect him from those who defame him personally or agitate against his overtures of peace and goodwill. We've probably all felt the wounds of someone's lying lips that left us feeling helpless and sputtering, the fire of our good intentions stamped out and left to smolder. *"What can I say, Lord? What can I do to combat these lies? Vindicate me! Preserve me and my good reputation!"*

Perhaps there is an additional way to pray this psalm: *"Lord, save me from (my own) lying lips and deceitful tongue."*

I am wounded and corrupted by my own deceit that tries to paint a glossy veneer over my own habits. I twist a few words, and suddenly I've created a fantastical reality that avoids pinpointing my own culpability for hurting others and not *actually* living for God.

What to do? Ask God to deliver us from the sins of others. Ask him to show a way forward to resolution and forgiveness. The Holy Spirit works continually, revealing our own deceptions that prevent cleansing light from shining on our internal messes. God's arms are open. He embraces us as we are. We are always forgiven. Each moment is a new beginning.

Learning to wait
Nathan Nass

God likes to make people wait. Have you noticed that? When you pray, you usually don't receive an answer right away. When you make plans, they often don't work out on your timetable. God likes to make people wait.

As Moses and the Israelites traveled to the Promised Land of Canaan, God set up an interesting system. When the cloud of his presence was over the tabernacle, the people had to wait. When the cloud set out from over the tabernacle, they could go. **"Sometimes the cloud stayed only from evening till morning, and when it lifted in the morning, they set out. Whether by day or by night, whenever the cloud lifted, they set out. Whether the cloud stayed over the tabernacle for two days or a month or a year, the Israelites would remain in camp and not set out; but when it lifted, they would set out"** (Numbers 9:21,22).

How would you have handled that? It sounds like a lot of waiting! What was God teaching his people? To depend completely on him. To trust completely in his plan and in his timing and in his will. That's why God likes to make people wait.

Believers waited thousands of years for the Savior—Jesus!—to come. Christians have waited two thousand years for Jesus to come again. All that waiting gives God's people a wonderful opportunity: to learn to depend on God, to learn to trust in God's promises. God likes to make people wait.

Give thanks to the Lord, for "it" is good
Jan Gompper

What if you woke up and all you had was what you were thankful for yesterday? Gulp! Depending on the day, I might find my storehouse empty. If you're like me, your prayer list is often more request oriented than thanks focused.

God doesn't *need* our thanks. Yet he directs us to be thankful or to have gratitude throughout Scripture.

Author Amy Morin cites the following scientifically proven benefits of expressing gratitude: It opens the door to relationships. It improves physical and psychological health. It improves sleep. It enhances empathy and reduces aggression. It improves self-esteem.*

The God we worship has commanded us to do something that would ultimately benefit us! So how does this list translate to us as Christians?

Giving God thanks strengthens our relationship with him, reminding us of our reliance on him for everything.

Expressing gratitude to God gives us peace. When we focus on how good God is, we worry less and feel less stressed.

When we are less stressed, we sleep more soundly.

Thanking God for *our* blessings inspires us to want to be a blessing to others.

Giving thanks to God reminds us of how cherished and loved by him we are.

"Give thanks to the LORD, for he [and it] **is good"** (Psalm 136:1).

* Amy Morin, "7 Scientifically Proven Benefits of Gratitude," *Psychology Today*, April 3, 2015, https://www.psychologytoday.com/us/blog/what-mentally-strong-people-dont-do/201504/7-scientifically-proven-benefits-of-gratitude.

Not guilty!
Paul Mattek

Guilt tormented me. I'd hear in church about Jesus taking away my guilt, but I'd still feel guilty. The more I tried not to feel guilty, the more I remembered the bad I'd done. I'd wonder, "Do I have a weak faith? If I believe, doesn't Jesus promise to take away my guilt?" Years of guilt-induced faith questioning went by, to the point that I let that guilt influence my identity and actions. If I was going to feel guilty anyway, why not just have fun doing bad stuff? So I did.

I wasn't giving God enough credit. He does more than deal with guilty feelings. He kills their cause—sin. He transforms our very identity and gives us a "not guilty" certificate to prove it. I love where the apostle Paul confidently says, **"God made him who had no sin to be sin for us, so that in him we might become the righteousness of God"** (2 Corinthians 5:21). Jesus earned our righteousness (made us right with God) by never sinning, voluntarily being killed as though he was the guiltiest sinner, and then rising from death like he just had a restful nap so he could hand his righteousness to us.

When I finally grasped this truth (thank you, Holy Spirit!), it was like blinders fell off my eyes, mind, and soul. Maybe that's what the guilt-ridden Saul, a.k.a. the apostle Paul, felt in Acts 9 (read it if you haven't!). Our memories might bring up the bad things we've done, but thanks to Jesus, God won't. His righteousness is now our identity.

God is nearer than you think
Dave Scharf

On September 11, 2001, terrorists attacked and brought down the twin towers of the World Trade Center in New York City. Those old enough to remember can likely tell you the place where they were when they heard the news. It was shockingly evil, even for our world. When God is mentioned in documentaries about that day, mourners often question why God was so far away. We might wonder it too in the more "minor" tragedies of our lives that feel major. But is God really so far away?

Moses asked, **"What other nation is so great as to have their gods near them the way the Lord our God is near us whenever we pray to him?"** (Deuteronomy 4:7). God is near. Your God came here to save us. Your life is now one filled with the assurance of heaven. Christ's life is your life . . . his death is your death . . . his resurrection is your resurrection. Who else can say that of their god?

God came so near that the virgin Mary felt his warm breath on her face. Lepers felt his touch. Children were held in the arms of the Almighty. Joseph of Arimathea wiped the blood off the King of kings. The disciple Thomas touched Jesus' wounds. God touched you with water and the Word in your baptism. His body and blood touch your lips for your forgiveness in the Lord's Supper. He listens to you when you pray. What God comes so near? Only Jesus.

What's doctrine?
Mike Novotny

Doctrine seems like a dirty word. When I recently typed "doctrine" into an internet search bar, Google responded with related words like *indoctrination, brainwashing,* and *propaganda.* Not exactly the words we most want in our lives!

But before you wash my mouth out with soap, let's slow down and define what doctrine is. Doctrine simply refers to a set of beliefs held by a group. If you and your friends believe that racism is wrong, then you have a specific doctrine. If you believe in racial equality so much that you try to persuade racists to change their ways, you, technically, are trying to "indoctrinate" them, that is, to get your "doctrine into" them.

The issue then isn't if you have doctrine but which doctrine you have. What exactly do you believe and why? When it comes to Jesus, heaven, religion, sexuality, abortion, or anything else, how did you come to your convictions? Did you absorb the opinion of your friends? Copycat your parents' beliefs? Trust it just because the pastor said it?

God encourages us, **"Watch your life and doctrine closely"** (1 Timothy 4:16). That's what I want to help you do in the days to come. Let's check out what the Word has to say about good doctrine, false doctrine, and how you can make sure that your doctrine is God's doctrine.

Sound doctrine
Mike Novotny

Nothing matters more than sound doctrine. Paul told Titus, **"[The pastor] must hold firmly to the trustworthy message as it has been taught, so that he can encourage others by sound doctrine and refute those who oppose it"** (Titus 1:9). That's not just essential for pastors. It's vital for all Christian people, including you.

"Sound" doctrine is a set of beliefs that come from God himself and, therefore, are good for your soul. You don't believe them because of your feelings or your friends or your family. No, you "hold firmly" to them, because a trustworthy God can always be trusted. When you can back up your beliefs with the Bible, you know what you believe is good for your soul, because it comes from the God who knows what is best for your soul.

The result? Encouragement. Those beliefs will give you courage to stand strong when the world strays from God's truth and courage to run to Jesus when you have strayed into sin. Those same beliefs will be your source of encouragement for others, the truth you text to an anxious friend before her job interview or the hope you give to a dying father lying in a hospice bed.

I love sound doctrine. It comes from God's heart and not my own. That's why you can trust it. That's why you can encourage others with it.

Watch closely!
Mike Novotny

I was trying to buy some camping gear for a family vacation, and I found a website with unbelievable prices. There was the fancy sleeping bag I wanted at less than half the price of anywhere else, so I added it to my cart, typed in my debit card, and bought it before they sold out. Then I kept finding crazy deals—camping mats, camping stoves, and camping everything at insane rates. Add to cart! Add to cart! But before I sealed the deal with my last click, my wife said, "Hold up. I think this website might be fake." I leaned into my laptop and, for the first time, paid attention to the details. The typos. The grammatical errors. The misplaced logo. Weeks later, 16 unexpected charges from Singapore showed up on my card. I had been scammed.

What happened? How did I miss the clues right there in front of me? Simple. I stopped watching closely because someone told me exactly what I wanted to hear.

No wonder Paul wrote, **"The time will come when people will not put up with sound doctrine. Instead, to suit their own desires, they will gather around them a great number of teachers to say what their itching ears want to hear"** (2 Timothy 4:3). There are plenty of teachers who will offer you an exciting and convenient path to God ("No repentance required! Be you! Do you! And get God too!").

Don't make the mistake I made. **"Watch your . . . doctrine closely"** (1 Timothy 4:16).

Something more
Mike Novotny

At the seminary that I attended, there is a Greek phrase in big letters over the doors of the chapel where future pastors gather for worship: κηρύξατε τὸ εὐαγγέλιον. That first word means "Preach!" It's a message that comes with authority and not merely personal opinion, like messengers sent from the king to notify the citizens of the kingdom. The last phrase means "the gospel." The good news. The declaration that our God did a very good thing for very bad people, sending his Son to save sinners for eternal life.

Some people cringe over words like *preach* and *doctrine*. Not me. We need forgiveness that is more than a human invention or a friend's opinion. No, we need a message that comes with authority and power, one that originated at the throne of the God who will judge the living and the dead. Only something that big could calm our troubled hearts and assure us that we will, without a doubt, see the face of God.

"Preach the gospel," Jesus commanded to his church (Mark 16:15). Give them good doctrine, a message of love from the God of power, grace declared with authority.

Please don't get suckered into the shallow doctrine of 21st-century America, which idolizes human emotion and opinion and "my truth." Your soul needs something more. Listen to gospel preaching. Submit to the Bible's authority. The result is that the good news of Jesus will get the final word over your soul. And his truth will set you free.

Psalm 144 is for *you*
Linda Buxa

"Praise be to the Lord my Rock, who trains my hands for war, my fingers for battle. He is my loving God and my fortress, my stronghold and my deliverer, my shield, in whom I take refuge. . . . Lord, what are human beings that you care for them, mere mortals that you think of them? Reach down your hand from on high; deliver me and rescue me from the mighty waters. . . . Blessed is the people whose God is the Lord" (Psalm 144:1-3,7,15).

Though King David wrote this poem two thousand years ago, I can't help but think it was written for me—and you. We all need the reminder that the same God who prepared and trained David is our God too. He fights for us in every battle we face. He is faithful, even when we are not. He is love, absolutely and completely. He is our shield, protecting us when we have to fight. He is our fortress, sheltering us when we need to rest.

What are you that he cares for you? You are fearfully and wonderfully made. And because he loves you, Jesus became human to wage war against Satan for you. All because you—little you in the scheme of the whole vast universe—are so very worth fighting for. Blessed are you, because God is *your* Lord!

P.S. I encourage you to read all of Psalm 144. There just wasn't enough space today to comment on it all.

How you compare
Matt Ewart

After a person has been on this earth for about 12 years, a simple yet startling realization begins to take root in their mind: "I am my own person."

Along with this realization comes a question that will take at least another 12 years to begin to answer: "What kind of person am I?"

The way we tend to find an answer is by comparing ourselves to the people around us. We try to determine whom we are like. We pay attention to who likes us. We yearn to find a group of people that is like us.

But look at what God did in the beginning. When God set out to design humankind, he didn't identify us in how we compare to other people. And he certainly didn't identify us in how we compare to animals. Here's what he said in Genesis 1:26: **"Let us make mankind in our image, in our likeness."**

In the beginning, the only way to determine our identity was in comparison to God. The one we were most like was God himself.

What might surprise you is that this is still true today. Though we lost God's likeness because of sin, it has been restored to us. Jesus became the likeness of sinful mankind so that God's likeness would be restored to us by faith in Jesus.

So when you begin to wonder what kind of person you are, don't look around you. Just look at Jesus.

The best reunion
Ann Jahns

Does your family love reunions? Are you the family that gathers at the same place each year, sporting brightly colored matching T-shirts and bonding over food and games and crafts? Or maybe if your family does have a reunion, you conveniently have another obligation that day that you simply can't get out of. Because of past hurts, purposefully spending time with your family is far too painful.

Regardless of your personal family situation, I hope you remember that you are part of a larger family: God's family. Through your faith in Jesus, purchased and won by his sacrifice on a cross, his blood now flows through your veins. You may not be able to choose your earthly family, but your Father God has chosen you for his eternal one: **"For he chose us in him before the creation of the world to be holy and blameless in his sight. In love he predestined us for adoption to sonship through Jesus Christ"** (Ephesians 1:4,5).

And what a glorious family reunion awaits us in heaven! Can you picture it? The apostle John describes it in the stunning vision God gave him of heaven: **"There before me was a great multitude that no one could count, from every nation, tribe, people and language. . . . They cried out in a loud voice: 'Salvation belongs to our God, who sits on the throne, and to the Lamb'"** (Revelation 7:9,10).

What a family reunion that will be. Whom can you invite to God's eternal family reunion?

God's Word is a treasure
Clark Schultz

While traveling, in addition to waking everyone else up in the hotel, our boys love to fight over elevator buttons, key fobs to open doors, and the chance to rummage through all the drawers and closets for treasure.

While pillaging room 523 in Cleveland, the boys discovered a Bible and asked, "Dad, someone left their Bible here. Who would do that?" This led to a discussion of who Gideon is and the practice of hotels leaving a Bible in every room.

Then while taking a trip to the Rock & Roll Hall of Fame, another Bible observation was made. The King of Rock's Bible was behind glass for all to see. One of my sons said, "Dad, how can anyone read it if its behind glass?" Great point.

Quick! Tell me right now where your Bible is? Do you know?

First, I commend you for taking the time to pick up this devotional. However, it is not this devotional that will save you. It's only Jesus, found in the treasure of God's Word.

There is an old phrase by Charles Spurgeon that goes like this: "A Bible that's falling apart usually belongs to someone who isn't."

Continue to feed your faith on these devotions, and instead of using the Bible as a drink coaster, continue to explore it like a child looking for treasure. **"Devote yourself to the public reading of Scripture"** (1 Timothy 4:13).

Offering your whole life
Dave Scharf

Whom do you want to please in life? I would guess it is someone you are grateful to or for. The same is true in our relationship with our heavenly Father. Romans 12:1 says, **"Therefore, I urge you, brothers and sisters, in view of God's mercy, to offer your bodies as a living sacrifice, holy and pleasing to God—this is your true and proper worship."**

Paul describes an Old Testament burnt offering. Imagine you are an Israelite. You pick out your best sheep, the priest examines it, and then you slit the lamb's throat. The priest catches its lifeblood in a bowl and sprinkles it on all sides of God's altar as the sheep is burnt until it's nothing more than ash. You just made a burnt offering. But you didn't have to do it. There is no payment for sin in this offering, just thanks. It symbolizes your complete devotion to God.

Some might ask, "Why?" Go back to the altar. This time go to the altar of the cross and see the sacrifice being offered there. Jesus covers your sin and says, "We're at peace. There is no cost for you to pay." That's mercy. Jesus, the Lamb of God, sweeps all the dead sheep off the altar of God to make room for you to be a living sacrifice until the day he calls you home. That's mercy. Now in view of that mercy, what do you want to do? Offer your whole life.

Our self-sufficient God
Katrina Harrmann

When my family hikes into the woods, we take along 200 lbs. of "stuff." It's *necessary* stuff, like food, shelter, a stove, and water, but it's stuff, nonetheless. Whenever we strap on our 50-lb packs and lumber into the woods like cumbersome turtles with our homes on our backs, it reminds me of how needy we are as humans. And as we start to run out of supplies on the last day, I confess to feeling a bit nervous!

We were not created to be self-sufficient. Not in the least. That's more and more obvious these days when just about anything you could ask for can be delivered to your doorstep within 24 hours at the touch of a button.

We are needy. God is not. God doesn't have to worry about running out of anything that he lacks, because he lacks nothing! **"Ah, Sovereign Lord, you have made the heavens and the earth by your great power and outstretched arm. Nothing is too hard for you"** (Jeremiah 32:17).

We are the exact opposite. We were designed to need God. And only he can meet all our needs—including the most important need: salvation through Christ Jesus. I don't know about you, but the idea of a self-sufficient God gives me *great* comfort. He will always be enough. And he always gives us what we need!

A walking companion
Andrea Delwiche

Psalm 121 is one of the traveling songs of Israel. These psalms were walking companions, providing stability, meaning, rhythm, and heart's ease for the traveler. For travelers back then and for us today, what we learn by heart offers to go everywhere with us to keep us steady. Scripture can provide the rhythm for our walking—both in our literal daily walk and our life journey. Sit with these words and create a picture of them in your mind.

"I lift up my eyes to the hills. From where does my help come? My help comes from the Lord, who made heaven and earth. He will not let your foot be moved; he who keeps you will not slumber. Behold, he who keeps Israel will neither slumber nor sleep. The Lord is your keeper; the Lord is your shade on your right hand. The sun shall not strike you by day, nor the moon by night. The Lord will keep you from all evil; he will keep your life. The Lord will keep your going out and your coming in from this time forth and forevermore" (verses 1–8 ESV).

Good techniques for memorization include carrying a passage in your pocket to read throughout the day. You can write the passage on a wide rubber band and wear it. Be sure to connect the Scripture to your life in a prayerful way.

Jesus himself taught, **"Out of the abundance of the heart the mouth speaks"** (Matthew 12:34 ESV). How could memorizing even this one psalm bring you peace?

God's piggyback ride
Nathan Nass

For a short window of time, a child gets a special treat: piggyback rides! Remember those? Every kid loves piggyback rides. From their parents' shoulders, they get to see the world from on high, feel extra safe, and rest their little legs. Nothing makes a child feel as special as when they get a piggyback ride from their mom or dad.

But you don't get piggyback rides for very long. Soon you grow too big for your parents to carry you. For the rest of your life, you have to navigate life on your own two feet. Aren't there days when you wish you could go back? When you wish you could rest on Mom's or Dad's shoulders again?

Then listen to God's invitation: **"Let the beloved of the Lord rest secure in him, for he shields him all day long, and the one the Lord loves rests between his shoulders"** (Deuteronomy 33:12). Those words were spoken to the tribe of Benjamin in ancient Israel. They lived in the mountains, as if they were resting securely on someone's shoulders. But those mountains didn't provide their security. The Lord did!

Just like he does for you. You are never too big to ride on God's shoulders. He's strong enough to carry you, even with all your baggage and sins and worries and fears. Jesus gives forgiveness and strength. God your Father loves to swing you up on his shoulders and carry you. "The one the Lord loves rests between his shoulders." It's God's lifelong piggyback ride.

No exceptions
Liz Schroeder

My inner lawyer doesn't have my best interest at heart. When I'm tempted to go against the will of God, my inner lawyer is quick to soothe me. *"Sure, God said to be self-controlled and alert, but after the day you had, you deserve to let loose and tune out your responsibilities. You're the exception to the law,"* he croons.

Like a two-faced mythical beast, that same lawyer turns his argument around after I've sinned. *"Look at what you've done,"* he tsks, pushing my nose into my mess like a cruel master to a dog. *"Who could ever forgive you? This 'merciful God' you claim to worship certainly has his limits; it's not like this is your first offense. 'God so loved the world'?"* he sneers. *"Surely you're the exception."*

If my inner lawyer sounds like yours, it's because he's been using the same tactics since the Garden of Eden. His croon-and-tsk combo worked so well on Adam and Eve that he tried it in the wilderness on our Savior. But this time his strategy didn't work. When the tempter twisted Scripture to entice Jesus to sin, Jesus wielded the Word of God to combat the tempter.

Whether your inner lawyer argues that you're the exception to the law or to the gospel, wield this: **"For everyone has sinned; we all fall short of God's glorious standard. Yet God, in his grace, freely makes us right in his sight. He did this through Christ Jesus when he freed us from the penalty for our sins"** (Romans 3:23,24 NLT). No exceptions.

No filter with the gospel!
Dave Scharf

Have you ever noticed that little children have no filter? If you have a big pimple on your face, they are going to point it out! My wife once asked one of our daughters how she looked in a dress, and my daughter said, "The dress makes you look young, but your face makes you look old." ☺

But that lack of filter is a wonderful quality for sharing the gospel. Think of how loudly young children pray in a restaurant while their parents mumble. When children sing in church, they belt out their praises! Children are not ashamed to proclaim the gospel. Why? Because it's true and important! They genuinely care about other people and want them in heaven. How quickly we lose that quality and start thinking about how proclaiming the soul-saving gospel might affect the way people think of us.

The apostle Paul tells us to stop being so grown up and get back to our childlike ways! He says, **"I am not ashamed of the gospel, because it is the power of God that brings salvation to everyone who believes"** (Romans 1:16). Remember that this good news changed your life. Remember that someone was unashamed to tell you about Jesus' love for you on the cross. Remember what you want for every person you meet: for this person to be in heaven with you. Remember that this message is God's power to change hearts. There's no need for a filter with the gospel!

Quietly present
Clark Schultz

Who is your best friend? Why? Do you have too many to count? If you hit a rough patch or need to make a serious decision, who do you ring, text, or snap to give you the wise counsel you need?

To me, one characteristic of a good friend is that they keep their mouths shut when it matters. When visiting someone with a hurting heart, I've been guilty of being "that friend"—the one who spews out all the 50-plus years of knowledge I have, fires a few Bible passages at them, and gives them a diatribe of wisdom. Wrong approach. A true friend is one who is there with you quietly in the moment.

When my brother was killed tragically in a snowmobile accident at a young age, my world was rocked. Some people didn't know what to say or what to do. Due to the stages of grief I was going through, folks who were "that friend" with all the words made me want to punch them in the face. But the most memorable moment for me was when a group of my friends came over and we all just sat in silence. No words, just their presence was soothing to my hurting heart.

Jesus, our best Friend, invites us to come to him in those moments as well. He says, **"Come to me all you who are weary and burdened"** (Matthew 11:28). Whether you see him or not, Jesus is with you in the silence too. He is there; you are never alone.

Love one another
Andrea Delwiche

Today is a new day. Will it be defined by your unbeliev-able love for others? Think of the words Jesus spoke just after he had washed his disciples' feet and before he was betrayed to suffer and die: **"A new command I give you: Love one another. As I have loved you, so you must love one another. By this everyone will know that you are my disciples, if you love one another"** (John 13:34,35).

In Psalm 122, written centuries earlier, we hear about a demonstration of this same divine love principle: **"For the sake of my family and friends, I will say, 'Peace be within you.' For the sake of the house of the Lord our God, I will seek your prosperity"** (verses 8,9). The psalmist vowed to seek peace and prosperity for others, and so do we. This isn't easy. If it were, perhaps Jesus wouldn't have felt the need to make love the defining distinctive of being his follower.

There is a Christian saying that goes something like this: "My sister or brother is never my enemy." Picture the vast diversity within your family, community, coun-try of origin, and the Christian church scattered across the globe. For whom do you need to pray, setting aside personal differences or preferences to uphold Jesus' command to love and the biblical principle to pray for the peace of others?

We can ask God to guide us, praying this ancient prayer: *Lord, make me an instrument of your peace. Where there is hatred, let me sow love. Amen.*

Learning from sand cranes
Jan Gompper

One of my favorite things about living in Florida is watching the sand cranes. It's rare to see one walking by itself. They instinctively travel in pairs or groups of three to protect themselves from predators, power lines, or oncoming traffic. They also forage and feed together. It's common to see cars slow to a stop while a group of sand cranes slowly meanders across the street.

We can learn from sand cranes.

Most Americans have grown up thinking that independence and self-sufficiency are keys to survival. Even some Christians have the belief that all anyone needs is God to navigate life.

Neither is true. Not long after Adam took his first breath, God realized that **"it is not good for the man to be alone"** (Genesis 2:18). Though Adam had a direct one-on-one relationship with his Creator, God had also designed him with a *need* for relationship, not only with him but also with other human beings.

Knowing that God wired us for human relationship, one would think that Christians and Christian churches would make fostering relationships a high priority. Sadly, this is not always the case.

The early church in Acts 2:42-47 understood and practiced relational Christianity. They worshiped and prayed together. They looked out for one another's physical needs. They ate in each other's homes and enjoyed one another's company. They knew that spiritual predators were all around them, so they stuck together.

We can learn a lot from them . . . and sand cranes.

He drank the cup!
Jon Enter

In a garden called Gethsemane, Jesus prayed earnestly for the Father to take the "cup" from him. What's so bad about a cup? That depends on what's in the cup! So what was in the cup Jesus was praying about? The rebellion of Adam. The drunkenness of Noah. The lies of Abraham. The deceit of Jacob. The adultery of David. The greed of Matthew. The denial of Peter. The betrayal of Judas. The murder of Paul. All of it was in the cup. And more. The sins of my past and yours. They were in the cup! Those times we've given in to the devil's temptations. They were in there. All the guilt, all the godless acts, all the lies, all the lust, all that we've done.

Jesus remained perfectly pure and perfectly in tune with his Father's will. He prayed, **"*Abba*, Father, . . . everything is possible for you. Take this cup from me. Yet not what I will, but what you will"** (Mark 14:36). Jesus finished that prayer and drank the cup of God's wrath by dying on a cross for our sins.

Do you know what this means? When you fall into temptation, you still have a way out! Confess your sins to the Lord. When you're suffering the effects from falling prey to the devil, turn to Jesus. Turn to his power to remove temptation's lock on your heart. Turn to Jesus and be free!

Jesus needs to show up!
Linda Buxa

I recently started watching a TV series based on the biblical story of Jesus, but it also includes fictional stories and conversations. In every episode, I see the pain of the demon possessed, the outcast, the worried, the sick, the dying. Each time I see their struggles, I say, "I can't wait for Jesus to show up!" See, I know these Bible stories and how they end, so I get antsy for Jesus to come and set things right.

I feel the same way about real life. I see people who are struggling because they are estranged from family, lonely, been hurt by the church, been abandoned by a spouse, or are battling mental illness, and I think, "I can't wait for Jesus to show up!" I want him to make all things right.

And then I realize I know two truths. One, after Jesus conquered death and went back to prepare a place for us, he promised he would be with us to the very end of the age. So that means he is already here. He hasn't left us. He still cares about each of us and our problems and hurts.

Two, he promised he would show up again to take us to that place where all things are new, where there is no more crying or sickness or heartache or pain. And he gives us this promise to cling to: **"I am coming soon. Hold on to what you have, so that no one will take your crown"** (Revelation 3:11).

The fog of war
Liz Schroeder

Friends of ours use the term "the fog of war" to describe their season of raising grade school and high school children. Maybe you can relate. Driving one kid to practice, another to a game, and buying a gift for yet another birthday party—all while discipling their hearts, managing your work and home, and squeezing in an occasional date night so you don't forget the person you married.

Or maybe your fog of war looks a bit different. Taking your spouse to doctor visit after doctor visit, wrestling with insurance claims, wasting hours on hold with customer service—all while trying to preserve your spouse's dignity and your identity.

Whatever your fog looks like, the Bible tells us, **"For our struggle is not against flesh and blood, but against the rulers, against the authorities, against the powers of this dark world and against the spiritual forces of evil in the heavenly realms"** (Ephesians 6:12).

Though it might seem like you're fighting an administration, a boss, a spouse, or a rebellious teenager, it is a spiritual battle. And you can't bring an earthly weapon to a spiritual battle. Your strategy and charisma aren't going to cut it; you need the full armor of God.

"Therefore put on the full armor of God, so that when the day of evil comes, you may be able to stand your ground, and after you have done everything, to stand" (Ephesians 6:13).

The day is coming when the fog will be lifted, and we will stand with our Lord, victorious. Hang in there, soldier.

Strong in weakness
Paul Mattek

"Simon, Simon, Satan has asked to sift all of you as wheat" (Luke 22:31). That Bible passage terrified me at one point in my life when my faith was dry as a bone and nothing seemed to restore it. But at that point, the more I tried, the further my faith went numb and an indescribable terror overtook me.

Satan was sifting me like wheat, and there wasn't anything I could do to stop it. So I fell on my face and submitted to the inevitable. "OK, Lord, if this was what was supposed to be, then I guess I'm a Judas or one of the multitude of horrible kings of Israel and Judah who had your prophetic words spoken to them and didn't listen. You probably knew this about me from the moment I was born." I sat with that for a while and closed my eyes. I didn't want a friend to talk me out of these thoughts. I didn't want to do anything.

But God tapped my memory with the next verse: **"But I have prayed for you"** (verse 32). And then he tapped again with John 17:20-26, where Jesus prays for all believers.

God reminded me that I don't stand a chance when it's me versus the devil. He reminded me that I can't do anything on my own. I need him. He took on the devil and won.

And it was then that I finally knew what another verse meant: **"When I am weak, then I am strong"** (2 Corinthians 12:10).

AUGUST

Confess your sins to each other and pray for each
other so that you may be healed. The prayer of a
righteous person is powerful and effective.

JAMES 5:16

More than a big fish
Mike Novotny

Don't get distracted by the big fish, because the book of Jonah is really about a big God. If you know anything about this four-chapter book tucked near the end of the Old Testament, it's probably about the giant fish that swallowed ol' Jonah, but the fish is only mentioned three times. Jonah himself is mentioned 18 times, but even he is not the star of this story. That honor belongs to the God who is mentioned 40 times in this 48-verse book!

To be more specific, the book of Jonah is about God's love for all people. From the violent, wicked, and abusive Assyrians to the self-righteous, pouty, holier-than-thou Jonah, God shows his shocking love for all kinds of people before the book is done. We see hints of that love in the very first verses: **"The word of the Lord came to Jonah son of Amittai: 'Go to the great city of Nineveh'"** (Jonah 1:1,2). The Lord told a Torah-loving Jew from a small town near Nazareth to take a mission trip to a metropolitan, Gentile, pagan city. Why? Because God, as John later pointed out, loves the world (John 3:16).

If you struggle with loving "those people" or believing that God loves you, keep reading the book of Jonah. And don't get distracted by the big fish! This book is about the even bigger love that God has for the world.

God loves *all* people
Mike Novotny

Why would Jonah run? **"The word of the** Lord **came to Jonah son of Amittai: 'Go to the great city of Nineveh and preach against it, because its wickedness has come up before me.' But Jonah ran away from the** Lord**"** (Jonah 1:1-3). Running from the Lord who is everywhere all the time is about as dumb as Adam and Eve trying to hide from the God who is always behind every tree. Why did Jonah do it?

You might assume he was afraid. After all, Nineveh was known for decapitating, impaling, and peeling the skin off of its enemies. Would you want to march up and down its streets all alone, preaching fire and brimstone? Spoiler alert!—Jonah didn't run out of fear of being flayed. He ran out of fear that God would forgive. This prophet knew enough about God's character that if, by some miracle, the people of Nineveh would repent, the Lord would certainly relent. He would save them by grace. That thought—"those people" saved—was so abhorrent that Jonah sprinted in the opposite direction of God's call.

Is there anyone you know whom you wouldn't want to be saved? As we journey deeper into the book of Jonah, wrestle with these questions: Who don't you pray for? Who wouldn't you share the gospel with? And why? I pray that this book, saturated with God's love for the world (and you!), inspires you to love the world too.

Follow Jesus' example
Mike Novotny

Why did God bother with Jonah, the runaway, rebellious, self-righteous prophet? When Jonah **"ran away from the Lord"** (Jonah 1:3), why didn't God just let him run? Or let him drown in the storm? Why didn't God tell the angels to find a new prophet? Simple. Because God loves "those people."

I had to wrestle with that fact earlier this year. Recently, I had a request to do an interview with a Christian group whose social media pages rubbed me the wrong way. Post after post was about "those people" who are the real problem with America. Article after article was about "those people" whose sins are destroying this nation. It felt so pharisaical that I wanted to keep my distance from such folks.

But one day it hit me. Am I doing what Jesus did? When a tax collector invited Jesus over for dinner and his rule-breaking buddies were at the table, what did Jesus do? He went. He ate. He spoke the truth, and he spoke it in love. And when a Pharisee invited Jesus over for dinner and his rule-keeping but incredibly judgmental buddies were at the table, what did Jesus do? He went there too! He ate there too! He spoke the truth, and he spoke it in love there too!

Jesus embodied what the book of Jonah is all about, namely, God's love for all people. May we, full of grace and truth, be the next example of showing and sharing that love with the world.

Rock bottom prayers
Mike Novotny

Have you ever hit rock bottom? Like when people are telling you what you said at the party but you can't remember a word of it? Or when you are Googling "divorce lawyers in my area" for the very first time? Or when you think for the first time about why you do what you do and wonder how many of your "good works" have been fueled by bad motives?

Here's the tricky part: When you hit rock bottom, it's hard to reach out to the Most High God. As much as you need God, sometimes you don't run to him, because you feel so far from God. You wonder if he wants anything to do with you. You wonder if he's even listening. You're disgusted with yourself, so wouldn't a holy God who hates sin be even more disgusted? Why bother to ask him for help?

If that's you, here's what I want to tell you: God responds to rock bottom prayers. Even if it's your fault that you're there, God responds to rock bottom prayers. Even when you're that low, God will respond from on high. Here's the proof: **"From inside the fish Jonah prayed to the Lord his God"** (Jonah 2:1). Jonah, the rebellious, runaway prophet, prayed . . . and God answered!

There is no place, no matter how low, that is too far from the ears of God. Call out to him! Cry out for mercy! The God who loves the world, including those who've hit rock bottom, has promised to listen.

Turn to the Psalms
Mike Novotny

Unless you are an Old Testament scholar, you probably didn't know Jonah quoted so much Scripture. While inside a big fish, Jonah prayed, **"You hurled me into the depths, into the very heart of the seas, and the currents swirled about me; all your waves and breakers swept over me. I said, 'I have been banished from your sight; yet I will look again toward your holy temple.' The engulfing waters threatened me, the deep surrounded me; seaweed was wrapped around my head. To the roots of the mountains I sank down; the earth beneath barred me in forever. But you, Lord my God, brought my life up from the pit. When my life was ebbing away, I remembered you, Lord, and my prayer rose to you, to your holy temple"** (Jonah 2:3-7).

Almost every line of that prayer is a snippet from the Psalms—Psalms 30, 42, 5, 103, 18, and 107, proof that when you're in a dark place (pun intended), it's good to know your Bible. When life gets hard, there's no better place to turn than the Psalms.

Some Christians love to start their day with a chapter of Proverbs, since it's filled with wisdom to prepare you for the day ahead. I suggest you end your day with a chapter of Psalms, a book filled with the God who saves, who is our refuge, who hears our prayers, and who lifts us up, providing peace no matter what happened during our day. Be like Jonah today and spend some time in the saving words of the Psalms.

Joyful worship
Mike Novotny

How can you resist a sin that feels so good? How can you fight your critical nature or stay sober when everyone else isn't or love that tough-to-love person in your family? How can you give more money away or be courageous enough to stand up to your friends when they gossip? In other words, how can you follow God with a joyful, willing heart?

Jonah knows. **"Those who cling to worthless idols turn away from God's love for them. But I, with shouts of grateful praise, will sacrifice to you. What I have vowed I will make good. I will say, 'Salvation comes from the Lord'"** (Jonah 2:8,9). Why repent? Why obey?

First, so you don't "turn away from God's love." God loves the world, but you can turn away from that love if you "cling to" anything besides God. Is any sin worth throwing away his eternal love? Is any temporary thing worth more than being with God forever?

Second, because the Lord saved you. Jonah is shouting (not mumbling), is grateful (not grumbling), is ready to sacrifice to God. Why? Because "salvation comes from the Lord." That's the spiritual game changer! You made a mess, but God made you clean. You did the crime, but the cross did the time. You broke it, but your Father bought it. You were dead, but God made you alive. That salvation will change your heart and compel you to joyful worship.

Fix your eyes on the cost of sin and the cross of Jesus, and you will joyfully worship God too.

By God's grace
Mike Novotny

Can you think of someone who will never become a Christian? Someone so set in their ways and their sins that there is no chance they will repent and believe in the true God? Before you answer, check out what happened in Jonah chapter 3:

"Then the word of the Lord came to Jonah a second time: 'Go to the great city of Nineveh and proclaim to it the message I give you.' Jonah began by going a day's journey into the city, proclaiming, 'Forty more days and Nineveh will be overthrown'" (verses 1,2,4). Jonah walked into this ancient metropolis, famous for its wickedness, and turned over God's sand timer of judgment. "Forty days and you're dead!"

You would think that the next verse would say, "Then the men of Nineveh arrested, tortured, and murdered the prophet who dared to defy them." But that's not what the next verse says. Here's what it says: **"The Ninevites believed God"** (verse 5).

No. Way. Nineveh?! There wasn't a chance that people so bad could do something so good! But apparently, they did. The Holy Spirit can do more than we ask or imagine. Just ask Jonah!

There is no promise that everyone you love will be saved, but there is the potential. Don't stop praying. Don't stop loving. Maybe one day something will change, and God will grant them a change of heart. It happened back then, and by God's grace, it can still happen today.

What's repentance?
Mike Novotny

What is repentance? Is it something you feel? think? something you do? We can learn a lot by looking at the repentance described in the book of Jonah:

"The Ninevites believed God. A fast was proclaimed, and all of them, from the greatest to the least, put on sackcloth. When Jonah's warning reached the king of Nineveh, he rose from his throne, took off his royal robes, covered himself with sackcloth and sat down in the dust. This is the proclamation he issued in Nineveh: . . . 'Let everyone call urgently on God. Let them give up their evil ways and their violence. Who knows? God may yet relent and with compassion turn from his fierce anger so that we will not perish'" (Jonah 3:5-9).

In this crash course on repentance, we learn a few key truths. First, repentant people are sorry for sin. They aren't proud of sin. They can't plan to live in sin. Next, repentant people show they are sorry. In this case, it was fasting and sackcloth. In other passages, this is called the fruit of repentance, the visible proof that we are sorry for our sins. Finally, repentant people call on God's compassion. They know they deserve his anger, justice, and wrath, so they call on God's compassion, mercy, and grace. They look to his love to save them from their sins.

You may not be wearing sackcloth today, but a repentant heart is sorry for sin, focused on Jesus' forgiveness, and willing to make necessary changes. May God give all of us humble, repentant hearts.

God's abounding love
Mike Novotny

If you have trouble forgiving yourself or believing that God isn't mad at you after you messed up in a big way, look at how God treated the wicked people of Nineveh after they repented. **"When God saw what they did and how they turned from their evil ways, he relented and did not bring on them the destruction he had threatened"** (Jonah 3:10). Despite their countless sins, God immediately showed them mercy.

By nature, we tend to think of our relationship with God as a scale that balances good and bad choices. If we do more good things than bad things, God smiles. If we do more bad things than good things, God scowls. So if you've done too many bad things, you better pile up some good things before God brings destruction down on your head.

But that isn't true, and this story is the proof. God relented before these sinners had time to put in much effort. Their hearts turned from sin and turned to him, and—boom!—God showed compassion, a preview of how Jesus would later treat the thief on the cross.

The Lord treats you the same way. You might think you have to earn back God's love, but you don't. You might assume you need some time to balance the scales and be worthy of his affection, but you don't. Because God is God—abounding in love and full of grace—you can run back to him in repentance any time, on any day, and find his arms wide open.

Isn't grace amazing?

Angry at God
Mike Novotny

A few months ago, I reached out to a Christian counselor and asked, "What makes people get mad at God?" His answer? "Expectations." People have an idea about how God should act, and when God doesn't act like he "should," people get mad. I think he's right. For example, you might get mad at God when he allows more pain in your life than he "should."

Or like the prophet Jonah, you might get mad that God is so quick to forgive. After God's mercy on the wicked people of Nineveh, we read, **"But to Jonah this seemed very wrong, and he became angry"** (Jonah 4:1). Jonah was red in the face furious because he felt it was wrong for God to forgive "those people" who had no right to grace after committing such horrific wrongs.

Imagine someone who hurt you deeply showing up at church and sitting three rows in front of you. Imagine, even if they were sorry for their sin, how you would feel as the pastor says, "God loves you. God forgives you for everything. Because of Jesus, God isn't thinking about your sin. He likes you!" If you saw the one who wounded you nodding, wiping away a tear, and smiling at grace, would you grimace?

The final chapter of Jonah forces us to think deeply about God's grace toward those who have sinned against us. If they repent, do you want God to rescue them? Do you want them in heaven with you? Will it seem very wrong if they are right with God?

God's character
Mike Novotny

Do you know the most-quoted verse in the entire Old Testament, the one that shows up over 20 times throughout the Law, the Prophets, and the Psalms? Jonah did. In fact, he memorized it.

In the midst of his tantrum over God's love for the world, Jonah said, **"I knew that you are a gracious and compassionate God, slow to anger and abounding in love"** (Jonah 4:2). Those four descriptions of God come from a famous interaction between God and Moses in Exodus 34, where the Lord reveals what he's really like. Gracious—not punishing those who repent. Compassionate—blessing those who deserve to be cursed. Slow to anger—God takes a deep breath before his justice comes. Abounding in love—more acts of love than hairs on your head. God reveals the beautiful balance between his grace for his people and his justice upon those who do not repent.

My mom used to repeat before I went out with friends, "No drinking, no smoking, no sex, no drugs." My dad still repeats, "You don't know how good you got it." I repeat to my daughters, "You know God loves you, right?" And Jews would repeat, **"The Lord, the Lord, the compassionate and gracious God, slow to anger, and abounding in love"** (Exodus 34:6).

Got a few minutes today? Read—better yet, memorize—Exodus 34:6,7 and get to know the character of our God.

The heart of God
Mike Novotny

Imagine a spectrum of morality with the worst people on one end and the most-loving people on the other end. Moral monsters here; Mother Teresas there. From Hitler to child abusers to violent criminals to desperate addicts to the arrogant, the average, the kind, the generous, the good examples, the people you want to babysit your babies, and the people you want to be like. Can you picture a lineup of humanity according to morality?

Who has a chance of going to heaven? And who is in danger of the torment of hell? According to God, everyone and everyone. No one, according to Jesus, is so good they deserve to be with God. And no one, according to Jesus, is so bad they can't make it to God, can't be saved.

That is what made Jonah mad. After seeing the wicked men of Nineveh spared, he whined, **"I knew that you are a gracious and compassionate God, slow to anger and abounding in love, a God who relents from sending calamity. Now, LORD, take away my life, for it is better for me to die than to live"** (Jonah 4:2,3).

True Christianity is unbearable to some people, because salvation is not by works. Sin—every size and shape of it—is worse than you think, so bad that even the best life can't pay its debt. Grace—abounding in God's heart and poured out on the cross—is better than you believe, so good that even the worst sinners can be saved. Grasp that, and you'll get the heart of God.

At the heart of our emotions
Mike Novotny

The reason that the prophet Jonah was mad enough to run from God is that Jonah was infatuated with Jonah. Skim the final chapter of this Old Testament book, and you'll find plenty of "I" and "me" and "my" on Jonah's lips. To expose his self-centeredness, look what God did:

"Then the LORD **God provided a leafy plant and made it grow up over Jonah to give shade for his head to ease his discomfort, and Jonah was very happy about the plant. But at dawn the next day God provided a worm, which chewed the plant so that it withered. When the sun rose, God provided a scorching east wind, and the sun blazed on Jonah's head so that he grew faint. He wanted to die"** (Jonah 4:6-8).

Jonah was so angry about his sunburn that he wanted to die. But when God saved thousands of others from burning in hell, Jonah didn't care. Scratch that. Jonah claimed that God's grace had gone too far!

Take note of your strongest emotions today. What makes you angry? What triggers you to excessive reactions? Probe your emotions, and figure out what's at the heart of it. You, like Jonah, may be too interested in yourself and not interested enough in others. Drag that sin to Jesus. If there's anything we learn from the book of Jonah, it is that our God truly does love and forgive sinners like us.

The essence of our faith
Mike Novotny

Ready for a cliff-hanger? Here's how the book of Jonah ends: **"But the Lord said, 'You have been concerned about this plant, though you did not tend it or make it grow. It sprang up overnight and died overnight. And should I not have concern for the great city of Nineveh, in which there are more than a hundred and twenty thousand people who cannot tell their right hand from their left—and also many animals?'"** (Jonah 4:10,11). God said, "Jonah, you care about a little vine and some extra shade. Shouldn't I care about a big city and saving souls?"

That question hangs, unanswered, at the end of Jonah. How will Jonah answer? How will we? Will we have the humility to celebrate God's love for "those people"?

This story is not about a big fish but about the biggest issues of faith. It's about a God who really does love the world: violent Assyrians, self-righteous Jews, me, and you. It's about a God who calls people to repent, to be sorry for their sins, to show they are sorry for their sins. It's about a God who saves, who rescues pouty people who think they're good and wicked men who know they've been bad. It's about a God who would love the world so much that he would send his one and only Son that whoever believes in him—whoever!—would not perish but have eternal life.

Never mind the fish. Jonah is about the essence of our faith.

The flesh is weak
Jon Enter

When Jesus was tempted in Gethsemane not to drink the cup of God's judgment, his disciples were sleeping nearby. Jesus rose from prayer focused on completing the plan of salvation. He warned his disciples not to grow weary but to stay awake. They didn't. These words of Jesus are so often misunderstood. **"'Simon' he said to Peter, 'are you asleep? Couldn't you keep watch for one hour? Watch and pray so that you will not fall into temptation. The spirit is willing, but the flesh is weak'"** (Mark 14:37,38).

Many Christians hear those words and think they were spoken in disgust and anger. To hear Jesus say those words in that tone is a guilty conscience talking. Jesus had just left prayer in which he resolved himself to follow fully the Father's will of suffering alone and winning our salvation. Immediately, he was reminded why his death was needed. When Jesus said, "The spirit is willing, but the flesh is weak," he emphasized the first phrase. The disciples wanted to be faithful, but they couldn't.

Our spirit is willing and wanting to resist the devil, but our flesh is weak. So Jesus gives himself as our strength to resist temptation and be healed when we fail. That's why Jesus told the disciples and us what to do. "Watch and pray." Watch—be on your guard against the devil, knowing he will never stop tempting you. Then pray—rely on Jesus' forgiveness when you fail, knowing you are spiritually healed.

Our infinite God
Katrina Harrmann

Recently, I was looking at something I had made with my kids. "That was two years ago already," I commented to my husband. He looked at me. "Sweetie, that was like *five* years ago!" No way! We looked it up in the photo albums. Sure enough, it had been five years!

Looking at photo albums gives me a sense of time warp. Weren't my kids just five years old *yesterday*? Didn't we *just* take that vacation? And now my oldest is engaged!

Where does the time go?

Our God has control of our days. He is not intimidated or even concerned by the passing of years. He is outside of it, with his eyes on all our years at once—a staggering thought and yet one of immense comfort. Whom better to trust our futures and days with than the One who has a view of it all—from beginning to end?

"With the Lord a day is like a thousand years, and a thousand years are like a day" (2 Peter 3:8). Our infinite God sees time as we never will. What a blessing!

All we are asked to do is to be good stewards of the time God has given to us. So use your days wisely. Seek God's will in your daily walk, and when your own little fabric square of time doesn't make sense or baffles you, trust the God who holds the entire quilt in his hands, because he's fashioned it himself from day one and has a plan for each of our pieces in his masterpiece.

Struggling to pray?
Matt Ewart

"In Christ you have been brought to fullness" (Colossians 2:10).

If you are struggling to make prayer a regular part of your life, I could sit down with you over coffee and help you understand why it's a struggle. But before you even have time to put creamer in your coffee and stir it around, I could explain why you don't pray very often with one abrasive sentence—The reason you struggle to pray is because you believe there are better ways to spend your time.

You might believe that there are more productive ways to spend your time. Or you might believe that there are more fulfilling ways to spend your time. Or you might believe that there are more rewarding ways to spend your time.

The reason you don't spend time in prayer is because part of you believes what isn't true—that there are better ways to spend it.

And if I come off as judgmental or accusatory, just know that I'm writing this devotion for myself today. I need to hear this just as much as you do.

What we all need to hear is that Jesus loved us so much that he spent his time here on earth for us. He delighted in us, even as he prioritized the perfect prayer life with his Father.

Because of all he did, there is no more productive, fulfilling, or rewarding way to spend time than to think about God's presence and say, "Our Father in heaven . . ."

Nothing can separate you from God's love
Nathan Nass

Nothing can separate you from God's love. Do you believe that? It's hard. Sometimes we seem to be separated from God's love. Sometimes it seems like no one loves us at all. Sometimes our lives seem to scream out: "You are all alone!" You're not. Nothing can separate you from God's love.

Here's proof: **"I am convinced that neither death nor life, neither angels nor demons, neither the present nor the future, nor any powers, neither height nor depth, nor anything else in all creation, will be able to separate us from the love of God that is in Christ Jesus our Lord"** (Romans 8:38,39).

That's quite a list! Death, life, angels, demons . . . None of those can separate you from God's love! You could make your own list: depression, cancer, heartache, rejection, criticism, pain, old age, loneliness . . . Can any of those things separate you from God's love? No!

Because God's love is undeserved. It's not based on your behavior or your circumstances. It's based on Jesus, who lived, died, and rose for you. When you're good and when you're bad, God loves you. When life is good and when life is bad, God loves you.

Nothing can separate you from God's love. You need to hear that today. No matter what's going on in your life and in your head and in your heart, nothing will be able to separate you from the love of God that is in Christ Jesus.

Waiting for God
Andrea Delwiche

"I look to you, heaven-dwelling God, look up to you for help. Like servants, alert to their master's commands, like a maiden attending her lady, we're watching and waiting, holding our breath, awaiting your word of mercy" (Psalm 123:1-4 MSG).

Do you and I consider enough that we are God's creatures? Do we remember that our daily lives and breath are sustained by him? Think of a dog waiting with expectant eyes for a bite of food. Picture birds pecking around a bird feeder in the winter when seeds are scarce and buried under snow. We are like them, blessed to wait upon someone else for our daily bread. Our "heaven-dwelling God" answers our seeking eyes, hearts (and stomachs).

Jesus' own prayer teaches us to ask God to give us what we need for today. How would it change our scurrying lifestyles if we remembered that we are sustained by God's providence? He doesn't require us to neglect relationships, our own personal well-being, or our soul-tie with him to elbow our way through life.

This psalmist is also looking for physical protection. What if we relied more on God's protection and less on mustering our own resources for physical safety?

More of Jesus' words come to mind: **"Can any one of you by worrying add a single hour to your life?"** (Matthew 6:27). Better to use our time to meditate on God's promises than to chew on our problems. What does it look like for you and me to practice waiting for God—eyes lifted to heaven and palms outstretched in prayer?

Jesus is our everything
Clark Schultz

Want to find out who your true friends are? Make a mistake. I have noticed over the years that everyone loves you when you are on top of the mountain. I have also noticed the list of people dwindles greatly when you are kicked to the curb.

I have good friends, and I have best friends. The friends who've stood by me when my heart was broken are the same friends who stood by me when I watched my bride walk down the aisle. In both instances, they were there, not running the other way.

Recently, I took a police academy course. One of the police officers told the class, "When folks are running from the danger, we (the police) run to it to protect others." That made me realize who my best Friend is— Jesus. **"Cast all your anxiety on** [Jesus] **because he cares for you"** (1 Peter 5:7).

When others have turned their backs on me, he has not. When my sins have made a mess of life, Jesus reminds me that he took the full burden of my sins and yours to the cross with him. Will my life with Jesus be roses and grape Kool-Aid? No, in fact there will be ups and downs. The constant has and will always be my Friend and yours, Jesus. Some may say, "Is that all, just having Jesus as your friend?" That is not all; it is everything.

Serious sin, serious forgiveness
Dave Scharf

Have you lost the sense of seriousness about your sin? Have you been through the routine so many times that you've lost the realization of what sin does between you and God? It separates you. King David held on to his sins for nearly a year. This is what King David said it did to him: **"When I kept silent, my bones wasted away through my groaning all day long. Then I acknowledged my sin to you and did not cover up my iniquity. I said, 'I will confess my transgressions to the LORD.' And you forgave the guilt of my sin"** (Psalm 32:3,5). Are you holding on to a sin? Is it weighing heavily on you?

"Then I acknowledged my sin to you . . ." Admit that there is a clear standard. God's law is clear. " . . . and did not cover up my iniquity." Don't excuse your sin or shift the blame. Admit that you are the cause of your sin. "I said, 'I will confess my transgressions to the LORD.'" Notice this is not self-pity that hates the consequences of sin. Nor is this self-flagellation, hating yourself instead of your sin. This is sorrow for wronging your God. "And you forgave the guilt of my sin." Immediately, Jesus wraps you up in his arms and says, "I have loved you to hell and back on the cross. I will always love you. I could never love you more. You are forgiven." Take sin seriously, but just as seriously, rejoice in your forgiveness!

I am my brother's keeper
Ann Jahns

In 2023 the U.S. Surgeon General released a report. In the introduction, he talks about crossing the country and listening to Americans of all ages and backgrounds confess that they feel "isolated, invisible, and insignificant."*

People are lonely like never before. Despite our 24/7 digital connection, we are hungering for actual human connection. We want to know someone sees us—and cares.

In the book of Genesis, Cain's jealousy of his brother Abel eroded his heart. In a fit of rage, Cain murdered Abel and attempted to hide it from an all-knowing God. **"Then the Lord said to Cain, 'Where is your brother Abel?' 'I don't know,' he replied. 'Am I my brother's keeper?'"** (Genesis 4:9).

According to Jesus, Cain *was* his brother's keeper. So are we. After listing the most important commandment—loving God with all of our hearts—Jesus established the second most important commandment: **"Love your neighbor as yourself"** (Mark 12:31).

Our love of God and of our neighbor go hand in hand. I'm called to the privilege of being my brother's keeper. And my sister's. And my neighbor's. And my coworker's.

How can we show God's love to our neighbor? We can check in and ask questions. "God brought you to my mind today." "How can I pray for you?"

We can provide human connection and love. We can then let that love point our neighbor to Jesus.

* Dr. Vivek H. Murthy, "Our Epidemic of Loneliness and Isolation," https://www.hhs.gov/sites/default/files/surgeon-general-social-connection-advisory.pdf, 4.

Your guilt is gone
Paul Mattek

Confession time. Before I even reached puberty, I snuck my "girlfriend" into an empty church and kissed her. It was exhilarating for about 3.2 seconds . . . before guilt set in. This was not something the pastor would approve of. I knew because he was my dad. I deliberately did something forbidden. I told no one. For years, I hid it.

Perhaps you're hiding something too. Perhaps you see God as angry or your parents as disapproving, devoid of forgiveness and love. Perhaps you're used to a church culture where when you confess, no one forgives . . . unless you prove you are oh-so-very sorry first. Perhaps the thought of having to earn someone's forgiveness is too crushing, so you hide it.

You're not alone. David, a king of Israel, hid too. He committed an adulterous sin and then tried to cover it up with murder. It didn't work. His hidden guilt literally rotted his bones. But God reached out. In a gripping dialogue found in 2 Samuel 12, God sent a prophet named Nathan to draw David out of hiding with a pointed parable that confronted David with two very important truths: No sin is ever hidden from God, and guilt ends with God.

Psalm 32:5 recounts David's confession: **"Then I acknowledged my sin to you and did not cover up my iniquity. I said, 'I will confess my transgressions to the Lord.' And you forgave the guilt of my sin."** God knew David's sin and was more than ready to declare him not guilty!

Confess your sins to him. In Jesus, your guilt is gone too.

Let brotherly love continue
Jan Gompper

I recently had a conversation with a woman at church who had lost her husband in a tragic car accident. Through her tears, she told me she had been a member of our congregation for five years and that it wasn't until her husband died that anyone reached out to her. It grieved me to hear this, as I considered our church to be one of the friendliest I've ever attended.

While most churches offer warm smiles, handshakes, and even a free donut on Sunday mornings, it takes more than these to feel connected. The larger a church becomes the more isolated new people can feel. This doesn't mean we should avoid church growth, but perhaps we can do a better job of tuning in our radar to those most vulnerable.

Of course, getting connected is a two-way street. If people only show up on Sundays and don't get involved in church groups or activities, they will likely still feel isolated. Some people, however, just need a direct nudge, and it's not just up to church leaders to do the nudging.

Perhaps we start by inviting someone we don't know out for brunch after church, or we make an extra place at our holiday dinner table for that single or widowed person. How about asking a newcomer to go with us to a church or non-church event?

In whatever way possible, **"let brotherly love continue. Do not neglect to show hospitality to strangers, for thereby some have entertained angels unawares"** (Hebrews 13:1,2 ESV).

Do something or do nothing?
Matt Ewart

There are times when God calls on you to act. For example, he wants you to use your gifts in service to others. He wants you to be prepared to give a reason for the hope you have. He wants you to **"fight the good fight"** (1 Timothy 6:12).

But there are also times when God calls on you to do nothing. He wants you to be still and know that he is God. He wants you to know that there are some battles he fights for you—you need only be still. He wants you to watch what his mighty right arm can do.

So how do you know when to do something and when to do nothing? I would answer that by asking another question: Who is in control?

The apostle Peter thought nobody was in control when Jesus was about to be arrested, so he took matters into his own hands. He drew his sword and **"struck the servant of the high priest, cutting off his right ear"** (Luke 22:50).

In reality, when you read the account of Jesus' arrest, it is clear that Jesus was in control the entire time. He was asking the questions. He was guiding the outcome. So when Peter fought for control, he was resisting the One in control.

If Jesus was in control even in the darkest hour possible, he is in control of your circumstances too. Let that truth guide you to trust him, whether that means you do something or do nothing.

The main thing
Jon Enter

In Matthew 12, the Pharisees accused Jesus' disciples of breaking Sabbath law when they pulled heads of grain from a field and ate them. Jesus called his disciples innocent because they broke the rules, or traditions, of the Pharisees, not God's law. What made the Pharisees' tradition wrong was that they demanded the Jews *must* observe their tradition in order to follow God properly. Jesus disagreed.

There are traditions in Christian churches too. Traditions are good if they draw a believer's focus to Jesus, but traditions become wrong when they are demanded as the only way to worship and honor Jesus. Over one hundred years ago, churches and families split over whether to continue Lutheran worship in German or switch to English. Debates raged over the traditional version of the Lord's Prayer or the version without *thy*. Is it right for the pastor to wear a gown or not? Is music best on organ, piano, or with a worship band? Should there be worship screens or not? These questions have divided Jesus-loving Christians, leading to some awful words and accusations. When we turn something of worship into the main thing of worship, we fail.

"Worship the Lord your God, and serve him only" (Matthew 4:10). Worship is about Jesus. It's about realigning our hearts and lives to his will, not ours. The devil wins when he divides our hearts against each other over tradition or pushes our hearts from worship because of our preferences. How have you made worship about you?

The everlasting arms
Nathan Nass

It seems like everything is falling apart, doesn't it? When you look at the world . . . When you look at your own life . . . Who is holding all this together? Doesn't it seem like everything is falling apart?

It's not. It can't. Oh sure, bad things can happen and will happen. But everything isn't falling apart. It can't. Know why? **"The eternal God is your refuge, and underneath are the everlasting arms"** (Deuteronomy 33:27). The world isn't held together by chance or luck or some unknown force. The world—and your life—are held together by the everlasting arms of God. He is our refuge!

Even in death. Those words from the Bible are some of the last words of Moses, the great prophet who led God's people out of Egypt to the Promised Land. Even in death, Moses had confidence in the Lord. When human strength gives out, when there's nothing left that you can do, it's okay! Life doesn't depend on your strength. "The eternal God is your refuge, and underneath are the everlasting arms."

Jesus adds one more incredible detail to that picture. The arms that hold your life together have nail holes in them. Why? Because Jesus gave his life for you. To forgive all your sins. To win eternal life for you. The everlasting arms that hold the world together were once stretched out on a cross to save you. So no matter how life looks today, trust this: "underneath are the everlasting arms."

Muttering day and night
Linda Buxa

People who talk to themselves are usually considered a little crazy, right? (Although some say you aren't crazy unless you answer yourself.) But Psalm 1 has a different idea. It says people who talk to themselves are blessed. See for yourself: **"Blessed is the one . . . whose delight is in the law of the L**ord**, and who meditates on his law day and night. That person is like a tree planted by streams of water, which yields its fruit in season and whose leaf does not wither—whatever they do prospers"** (Psalm 1:1-3).

The day I learned that in Hebrew *meditate* means "to mutter" or "speak quietly," I muttered this psalm to myself. It changed so much. See, it's easy for my mind to get distracted as I'm looking at the words or skimming them. Muttering helps me slow down and read each word. The bonus is that the Bible promises blessings on the one who meditates day and night—and I like God's blessings.

It also makes me think about how we could mutter Scripture to ourselves all day.

When we're frustrated with people, we can mutter that love keeps no record of wrongs. When we're feeling alone, we can tell ourselves that God is always with us. When we are worried about our government, we can mutter that God is in charge. When we wonder about our purpose, we can remember that God sets the times and places where we live and that we are here to use our gifts for his glory.

What will you mutter today?

Your third strand
Liz Schroeder

On a hike through the foothills of the Sonoran Desert, I saw that a 20-foot saguaro cactus had keeled over. Nearby, a cluster of three saguaros stood tall. One had lost a limb, but they were otherwise thriving. This got me thinking about relationships, and Ecclesiastes 4:12 (NLT) came to mind.

"A person standing alone can be attacked and defeated." Your enemy cackles with glee when you self-isolate, which is fertile ground for pride, temptation, and loneliness. You're easy pickings.

"But two can stand back-to-back and conquer." When you're hiking through life with a Christian confidant or an accountability partner, you can go farther than when you go alone. Seek out someone who will encourage you toward holiness, not mere happiness. A prayer warrior and fellow soldier guarding your flank helps protect you from a sneak attack.

"Three are even better, for a triple-braided cord is not easily broken." As for the third strand, think honestly about your most important relationships: spouse, friend, roommate, sister, son. What is your third strand right now, the thing at the center of your relationship? Is it Netflix? A bottle of wine? A gym membership? Or is it growing in the grace of the Lord?

God doesn't tell you to put him at the center because he's desperate for attention. He tells you to put him at the center because he is the only being in the universe that can withstand the weight of your worship. Your spouse and kids can't. Your friends can't. Don't put that kind of weight on them. Instead, lean on Jesus and stand tall.

More than a name
Andrea Delwiche

"Our help is in the name of the Lord, the Maker of heaven and earth" (Psalm 124:8).

God's name is more than a name. God's name saves. God's name reveals his nature, power, reputation, and much more. Jesus spoke his name to a hostile crowd in the Garden of Gethsemane, and they fell backward to the ground.

We can't fully explain this mystery. But we can increase our understanding by spending time in holy wonder, contemplating a few examples.

"Save me, O God, by your name" (Psalm 54:1).

"Peter said, 'Silver or gold I do not have, but what I do have I give you. In the name of Jesus Christ of Nazareth, walk'" (Acts 3:6).

"God exalted him to the highest place and gave him the name that is above every name, that at the name of Jesus every knee should bow, in heaven and on earth and under the earth, and every tongue acknowledge that Jesus Christ is Lord, to the glory of God the Father" (Philippians 2:9-11).

"And this is his command: to believe in the name of his Son, Jesus Christ, and to love one another as he commanded us" (1 John 3:23).

How does God's power and goodness resonate today when we speak his name? Spend some time praying with and meditating on the name of Jesus. Imagine how joy echoes throughout heaven's courts when we speak God's name in trust. Ask the Spirit to lead you to a deeper understanding of all that is possible when you call on and believe in God's name.

You are not an orphan
Ann Jahns

Years ago I attended the funeral for the mom of a dear friend. Her mom had died unexpectedly, and my friend was still mourning the loss of her dad a few years prior. As my friend and I clung to each other in front of the casket, she whispered in my ear, "I am now an orphan." She was hurting because the two people who had loved her most in the world were now gone. She knew she wouldn't see them again until she too was taken to heaven.

As Jesus spent his final days with his disciples before his death, he spoke to them with an urgency that impending goodbyes bring. As he talked about leaving them to return to heaven, their hearts were heavy. They didn't understand why Jesus needed to leave. You can almost hear the hurt and confusion in Peter's voice: **"Lord, where are you going? . . . Why can't I follow you now?"** (John 13:36,37).

But Jesus wasn't leaving his friends to flounder alone. He gave them this assurance: **"I will not leave you as orphans; I will come to you. . . . You are in me, and I am in you"** (John 14:18,20). Jesus promised to send the Holy Spirit to empower them, to help them do the work he had prepared them to do.

You see, we are never truly orphans, even when our earthly parents pass away. Jesus lives in us. God, our heavenly Father, is our forever Father. And nothing—not even death—can separate us from his glorious presence.

SEPTEMBER

We live by faith, not by sight.

2 CORINTHIANS 5:7

Irresistible habits
Matt Ewart

Wouldn't it be nice if bad habits were easier to resist? And wouldn't it be nice if good habits were irresistible?

A mentor and friend of mine helped me understand why I was experiencing inconsistency when trying to implement new habits. It was not a matter of knowledge—I knew what to do. But knowledge did not make the new path irresistible.

The problem was not my mind but my heart. Specifically, my heart was believing something that made good habits way too resistible. I believed that today doesn't matter.

I had fallen for a lie. The truth is that the only day that I can work with is the today that God gives.

God is giving you another today, not just for your recreation or for your personal growth. He has a purpose for you that's bigger than this world. He has declared that you have a part in his story. His resurrection power is at work in you to transform your life to be like Christ. Through you, his light can shine in dark places.

If you've been wanting to develop new habits, align your heart to the truth of your God-given identity and purpose. That kind of good news is hard to resist.

"I will lead the blind by ways they have not known, along unfamiliar paths I will guide them; I will turn the darkness into light before them and make the rough places smooth. These are the things I will do; I will not forsake them" (Isaiah 42:16).

But to serve
Linda Buxa

One of Jesus' most well-known miracles is the feeding of five thousand people. (That's just men. Women and children were there too.) The people were hungry, but there wasn't enough food to feed everyone. A little boy shared his five loaves of bread and two fish. Jesus thanked God for the food, and the disciples handed it out. Everyone ate—and 12 basketfuls of food were left over.

It's easy to forget the context of this story though.

Jesus had *just* heard his cousin John had been murdered and, understandably, wanted privacy (maybe to grieve, to pray, to ponder his own death). So he took a boat to a secluded place, but the huge crowd walked to find him. When Jesus saw all of them, he didn't tell them to leave. Instead, he had compassion on them, healed them, and fed them.

Can you feel his humanity? The Son of Man was exhausted and grieving, yet he continued serving. Moments like this amaze me about my Lord and leave me speechless about my Savior. See, I usually just think about the big temptations he overcame but forget these "little" temptations too. He overcame the temptation not to serve, not to love. **"For even the Son of Man did not come to be served, but to serve, and to give his life as a ransom for many"** (Mark 10:45).

There's a lesson for us too when we face the temptation not to serve: **"Do not use your freedom to indulge the flesh; rather, serve one another humbly in love"** (Galatians 5:13).

I found what I'm looking for!
Dave Scharf

The band U2 has a song entitled, "I Still Haven't Found What I'm Looking For." You and I can relate. We go through life feeling like something is missing, fearing what will go wrong next. The women at the tomb on the first Easter didn't find what they were looking for either. They were looking for Jesus' body, but **"when they looked up, they saw that the stone . . . had been rolled away"** (Mark 16:4).

Have you ever wondered why the stone was rolled away? The stone was not rolled away so that Jesus could get out but so that the women could peek in! God's message was, "There's nothing to see here!" And that nothing changes everything!

You see, by finding nothing in the tomb, you find everything it is you are looking for in life because Jesus lives to give it. Are you looking for peace from a guilty conscience? Stop trying to get it by your own effort. The living Jesus says, "I give you a peace that passes all understanding." Are you looking for contentment? Stop trying to get it by getting more only to feel less content. The living Jesus says, "You have all you need in me and more." Are you looking for an answer to the grave? Stop looking for it in health programs and diets that only serve to stave off the inevitable. The living Jesus says, "See how my empty grave means yours will be too." I've finally found what I'm looking for! You too?

Our immeasurable God
Katrina Harrmann

Every year on the first day of school, we line our kiddos up and mark their heights against a wall, marking the passage of time and the growth of our family. I often get choked up looking at it, remembering the little people my kids once were.

As human beings, we're very measurable. We grow "this" tall. We are "this" many years old. We have "this" much patience and X amount of energy. We've been at our jobs X number of years, and those jobs start at a specific time on the clock each day.

One of the things that makes God GOD is that he is immeasurable. He is ageless and timeless. He has been at his "job" countless years. And he has infinite amounts of patience and love. We can't put him into a box with numbers and limits. We can't mark his height against a wall, and his love and patience are infinite. He is beyond all of our measuring and understanding.

"Great is our Lord and mighty in power; his understanding has no limit" (Psalm 147:5).

Wow. Our God is divine and powerful! So the next time you're frazzled because you're running late or don't have enough time in the day or feel like you're not measuring up, go to God and get everything you need to get through your measurable day and life, because he is your immeasurable Father.

September 5

Oh my God?
Jan Gompper

Oh my Buddha! My Brahma, did you see that accident? That movie was Allah-awful.

Do these phrases sound strange? Now substitute the name God. Sound a little more familiar?

Most of us likely learned this commandment: **"Thou shalt not take the name of the Lᴏʀᴅ thy God in vain"** (Exodus 20:7 KJV). More recently it's translated as, **"You shall not *misuse* the name of the Lᴏʀᴅ your God"** (NIV).

Church reformer Martin Luther expounded on the meaning of this commandment: *"We should fear and love God so that we do not curse, swear, use satanic arts, lie, or deceive by His name."**

You might be saying to yourself, "Okay, I get how all those things would be a 'misuse' of God's name. But 'Oh my God!' doesn't mean anything, does it?"

Aye, there's the rub.

I'm partial to the wording in the KJV: "Thou shalt not take the name of the Lᴏʀᴅ thy God *in vain*."

Webster's dictionary gives these synonyms for the phrase *in vain: unsuccessful, futile, useless, empty.* So saying God's name *in vain* means uttering it as if it has no value, purpose, or ability to accomplish anything. That's not what we mean to do, is it? And yet . . .

So how are we to use God's name? Martin Luther further elaborated that we are to *"call upon it in every trouble, pray, praise, and give thanks."*

Using God's name in these ways is never *in vain*.

* Martin Luther, *Luther's Small Catechism* (St. Louis: Concordia Publishing House, 2019), https://catechism.cph.org/en/10-commandments.html.

Through the pain
Paul Mattek

My two-year-old loves playing in puddles. She gets joy and contentment splish-splashing her hands and feet.

As adults, our default becomes skepticism and cynicism, not contentment. When we've experienced more pain than is "fair," we grumble, putting the burden of proof on others: "I've been burned before. Convince me otherwise."

Perhaps I can't convince you, but I can ask you to zoom out from your experience and realize what else isn't fair: that God had to give up his Son to brutal treatment and death.

Why? Because of pain—the pain of burying that parent whom you were starting to reconcile with, of having your church community reject you when you dared to bring a painful secret to them, the pain of mental anguish that doesn't let up, and the countless other horrible pains. It was never supposed to be this way.

But through, not around, the pain you'll find God's ultimate why: *you.* The Father, who has already shown how much worth you have by giving up his Son so that you can be with him, perfectly protected, content, and even able to have some splash-splash joy now, is here to guide you through the pain and loss. **"I consider that our present sufferings are not worth comparing with the glory that will be revealed in us"** (Romans 8:18). The pain is passing away; you are not! If you can believe that, you can live with contentment and joy even in the midst of pain and even be the hands that reach out, receive, and revive other pained people.

Where's your heart?
Jon Enter

Nobody has to tell you to honor the things that are important to you. You just do. If you're a sports fan, nobody has to tell you to turn on the game. You just do. When you hold your newborn child in your arms for the first time, nobody has to tell you to smile. You just do.

In Genesis 4, Cain and Abel offered God sacrifices, but only Abel's offering was accepted. In God's eyes, Cain wasn't giving an offering because it didn't come from his heart. Cain was just going through the motions. Jesus said it this way: **"Where your treasure is, there your heart will be also"** (Luke 12:34). In other words, the place where you direct your heart reveals exactly what your treasure is.

During the month, do you give more to God or streaming services? More to God or to eating out? More to God or your cell phone company? It's okay to have a hobby and spend money. It's okay to go to the mall or the movies. Yet if you turn your money over to those things happily but when it comes to turning it over to God, you hold on to it very tightly, then you're saying, "These things are worth it, but God isn't." And that's something God won't tolerate. What will it take for you to give offerings like Abel with a joyful heart?

Christianity is a relational religion
Mike Novotny

A few weeks ago, I was at a Christian musical festival where I saw a note stuck to the back of a minivan that read, "It's not a religion; it's a relationship." Have you ever heard that comment about Christianity?

It's kind of confusing, if you ask me. Because technically, isn't Christianity the world's largest religion? And doesn't that phrase encourage people to disconnect from church, accountability, and godly spiritual authority? And wasn't Jesus a fairly religious man himself, given his custom of going to the synagogue regularly (Luke 4:16)? On the other hand, didn't Jesus judge the religious Pharisees whom he claimed had no true relationship with the Father? And don't all of us know someone who goes to church but has no real connection to God?

Here's the biblical road between those two extremes, which I hope to explain in the devotions to come— Christianity is a relational religion. As James points out, there is a type of religion that **"God our Father accepts as pure and faultless"** (James 1:27). That religion follows the path of sacrificial love, a path we learn from our relationship with Jesus.

Don't let a sweet-sounding phrase pull you into an unhealthy place. Stay connected to church, pastoral leadership, and a community that provides accountability, *and* remember the God who is your Father and your friend. Because true Christianity is a relational religion.

Staying connected
Mike Novotny

Are you a religious person? I hope so. The word *religion* comes from a Latin word that means "to bind." True religion binds you to certain beliefs and behaviors that are outside of you. Instead of following their hearts/feelings/desires, religious people are bound to something unchanging, objective, and stable. That's why Christians don't get to invent their own list of Ten Commandments. We are, instead, bound to the list that our Lord already made.

Imagine holding a Bible and then having someone wrap a rope around both it and your hand. Thanks to that rope, you and the Bible would stay connected to each other, even if your grip started to slip. That, essentially, is what the Christian religion does. Weekly church services and other spiritual disciplines are the "rope of religion" that keeps you hearing God's commands and promises, even on those weeks when you are rather weak in your faith. Without religion, you might not hear the voice of your God at all.

No wonder the author to the Hebrews wrote, **"Let us hold unswervingly to the hope we profess, for he who promised is faithful. And let us consider how we may spur one another on toward love and good deeds, not giving up meeting together"** (10:23-25). Did you notice the connection between "meeting together" and our "hold" on the Christian hope? That's no coincidence. Because Christianity is a relational religion.

Don't run away!
Mike Novotny

Religion is unappealing to many people because of its rigid, restrictive nature. That's not an inaccurate description, because religion binds you to beliefs and behaviors that you don't get to choose or edit. You don't create your own commandments or design your personal path for salvation. Jesus is Lord and Savior, not you.

But this religion is for your good. I think of the Greek tale of Ulysses and the Sirens. Ulysses and his men were on a journey home after fighting in the Trojan War, but they had to pass by the Sirens, savage monsters who lured sailors toward their death-trap island with an irresistible song. Thankfully, Ulysses had been warned, so he ordered his men to tie him to the mast of his ship with ropes before plugging their own ears with wax.

As the temporarily deaf sailors sailed by, the Sirens sang their enchanting song, which was far more alluring than Ulysses could've imagined. Everything in him wanted to run toward the sound, but the ropes held him down and, in a way, saved him.

The Christian religion saves you too. James, in a chapter that mentions religion multiple times, writes, **"Humbly accept the word planted in you, which can save you"** (James 1:21). God's Word gets the last word over your heart, but that same word ties you to the comfort of the gospel when you feel unworthy, unlovable, and too sinful.

Don't run from religion. Bind yourself to God's Word and God's Word-bound people. That will keep you safe when temptation sings your name.

September 11

Partly religious?
Mike Novotny

Be careful with religion. Very, very, very careful with religion. Because people who are partly religious but not religious enough are a great danger to the name of Jesus.

You may recall that a religion is something that binds you to certain beliefs and behaviors. The problem, however, is when a person binds themselves to some but not all of what God has written in his Word. Picture a dad who goes to church and prays but then comes home and dominates his family with his rage. Or a pastor who compassionately counsels a hurting young woman but then crosses a line into inappropriate behavior. The problem in both of those examples is not that the father and the pastor are religious but that they aren't religious enough, not bound to the commands to be patient and pure.

James mentions this: **"Those who consider themselves religious and yet do not keep a tight rein on their tongues deceive themselves, and their religion is worthless"** (James 1:26). God has zero interest in a pick-and-choose version of Christianity. He wants his Word to get the last word over every area of our lives.

Is there any part of God's Book that your life is not bound to? Anything that God has said clearly that you've clearly skipped? Consider these questions carefully at the foot of the cross, where you can find forgiveness for every failure. Because your Father wants you to be *really* religious.

Treasured children of God
Mike Novotny

I love that Christianity is a relational religion. Yes, despite what some people say, the Christian faith is a religion, something that binds you to beliefs and behaviors outside of you. But please don't assume that makes it stiff, rigid, or boring. Because according to the very religious men who wrote the Bible, Christianity is a relational religion.

Listen to John, likely over 90 years old, gush about his religion: **"See what great love the Father has lavished on us, that we should be called children of God! And that is what we are!"** (1 John 3:1). As a father, there are few things I have ever loved in life more than my daughters. My affection for them could fill up oceans, which is why I lavish them with words and actions to prove my love.

The way God feels about you is even better than that. He doesn't just have love for you. John says that he has "great love." And he doesn't just give that great love to you. John says he "lavished" that love on you. Notice the double exclamation points in that single Bible verse. John can't believe that he, despite his sins, is a child of God!

And that is what you are too! Our religion binds us to a nearly unbelievable claim, convincing us of something we would never, ever assume to be true: We are holy, beloved, adored, cherished, treasured children of God.

Man, I love being religious!

God rejoices over you
Mike Novotny

My friend Paul got married last weekend. Paul is the goalkeeper on my soccer team, a tough dude you wouldn't want to mess with (especially in front of his net!). But last weekend as his soon-to-be wife, Allie, walked down their backyard aisle, I had my eyes on Paul. Like so many grooms before him, myself included, Paul was visibly emotional as he looked at his wife.

I love that moment, because Christianity compares it to our relationship with God. Isaiah writes, **"As a bridegroom** [a.k.a. groom] **rejoices over his bride, so will your God rejoice over you"** (Isaiah 62:5). Since Jesus dressed us in his perfection, we look more stunning to God than a bride does to her husband on their wedding day. I beg you not to miss the emotion in those verbs—God *rejoices* over you! He smiles, laughs, lights up with love visible in his eyes.

We live in a world that judges us by our works, which is why we rarely see that look in other people's eyes. We fall, fail, and fail to stand out from the crowd, causing others to look in the other direction. But the Christian religion binds us to the stunning belief that God is rejoicing over us with that wedding day look.

Can you even believe it?! It seems too good to be true, but the beautiful thing about being religious is that we are bound not to our thoughts and feelings but to the unchanging promises that God has made to us in Jesus. Rejoice today, my friend, because our God is rejoicing over you!

More than an hour on Sunday
Mike Novotny

Recently, my wife and I celebrated 20 years of marriage. To quote the classic film *Dumb and Dumber*, "I like her a lot." Our marriage isn't perfect, but it's really good. If you asked me why, I would tell you that a huge cause of our affection is how religious we are about date night. Every Friday from January through December, Kim and I try to go on a date. Since we both work, have two active kids, and have nearby parents whom we love, our schedules are busy, sometimes leaving us with less time together than we would prefer. But every Friday night gives us a weekly chance to reconnect and re-express our love for each other.

Sound familiar? Christianity commands us to **"not** [give] **up meeting together, as some are in the habit of doing,"** but rather to regularly gather week after week with our fellow believers (Hebrews 10:25). Why? There are many reasons, but perhaps the simplest is so you and God can reconnect at least once a week. Christianity is much more than an hour on Sunday, of course, but like my date night, church gives you a chance to affirm your love for God and for God to express his love for you.

Be religious about your Christian religion, meeting together from January through December. That is one of God's best ways to remind of you of the good news that isn't too good to be true.

September 15

A work in progress
Nathan Nass

You are a work in progress. Do you realize that? Let me clarify. You are God's work in progress. Here's what Isaiah learned to say to God: **"You, Lord, are our Father. We are the clay, you are the potter; we are all the work of your hand"** (Isaiah 64:8). We are all God's work in progress.

A lot of our anxiety in life comes from a misunderstanding. We think that God is done with us. We think that we're looking at the finished product. We get it in our heads that once we grow up and become adults, God's work in us is over, right?

No! You're God's work in progress. You're not the finished product yet, and you won't be until you get to heaven. What you see in your life today is just one chapter on the way to eternity.

God is still forming you, like a potter forms clay. Whatever trial you're in the middle of today isn't the end of the story. God's refining you and leading you to trust in him. Whatever heartache you're experiencing today isn't going to last forever. God's cutting something away to one day reveal something even better. If it seems like there's got to be something more than what you see, there is!

You're a work in progress, God's work in progress. So say with faith, "You, Lord, are our Father. We are the clay, you are the potter; we are all the work of your hand."

Fulfillment, Simeon style
Paul Mattek

Art invites you to consider something familiar with new eyes. *Song of Simeon*, a picture drawn by artist Jason Jaspersen, opened mine. Tucked into the events surrounding Jesus' birth in Luke 2, an elderly man named Simeon appears and sings prophecies over the baby Jesus and his parents. Starkly rendered in white on a black canvas, Simeon's look pierces you with an array of emotions. Sure, there is joy that he is seeing the fulfillment of God's promises. But there is also pain, longing, realization, and wonder. I've read the story countless times without grasping the moment's enormity, which is displayed in Jaspersen's artwork.

God revealed to Simeon that he wouldn't die until he met Jesus. But those revelations also showed the pain and injustice the devil and his allies would inflict along the way. There would be hard questions and intense pain for Mary and Joseph, pain for hearts hiding deep secrets and doubts, and death for the child himself.

But with all that on his heart, Simeon still sang! Glory! Salvation! He knew that anything less than God's perfect fulfillment of these prophecies would leave us with the ultimate lack of fulfillment—death and eternity without God's love. So Simeon held his baby Messiah, sang praises and blessings, and was filled.

And you? Read the story in Luke 2 and believe that what Simeon beheld has been accomplished. See the wondrous, complex, eternal, and beautiful fulfillment of God's love in Jesus—ready to be held by you too.

That's what love does
Linda Buxa

My daughter and I were talking about ways that I serve people, and she admitted that she wasn't sure she could do that. I admitted that sometimes I prefer to stay home in stretchy pants, but I give up some of my time because "that's what love does."

I thought about that concept as I started looking at ways that other Christians serve.

With an attitude of "that's what love does," they take their dad to multiple doctor's appointments, they care for their medically needy child, and they have hard conversations about things that have eternal implications. Others spend money on charities that serve their communities, some spend time building relationships and loving their neighbors, and some spend time praying continually for family members who don't believe in Jesus.

By serving others, they live out the encouragement to **"follow God's example, therefore, as dearly loved children and walk in the way of love, just as Christ loved us and gave himself up for us as a fragrant offering and sacrifice to God"** (Ephesians 5:1,2).

Mind if we consider two takeaways?

One, take time to consider how you walk in the way of love. What ways do you serve that show others what love does? How can you use your time and gifts to bless others?

Two, as you see others living their lives as fragrant offerings and sacrifices to God, encourage them. Service and sacrifice aren't always easy, and God's dearly loved children could use some of your support as they walk in the way of love.

Ears to hear

Jan Gompper

Political leanings aside, I have a vivid memory of a 2008 presidential debate between John McCain and Barack Obama. What I remember most is how courteous Obama was whenever McCain was speaking. Not only did Obama not interrupt McCain; he also turned and gave McCain his full attention before offering any rebuttal.

We've moved a long way from this example. Perhaps, like me, you don't even like watching political debates anymore because of all the interrupting candidates do, so much so that you can't understand what anyone is saying.

It seems that listening, especially to those whose philosophies differ from our own, has become a lost courtesy—and not just in political arenas. Even in Christian circles, shouts of condemnation can sometimes drown out the cries for help.

All you need to do is read Scripture to find that this isn't a new phenomenon. Solomon warned, **"To answer before listening—that is folly and shame"** (Proverbs 18:13). And James the half brother of Jesus advised, **"Everyone should be quick to listen, slow to speak and slow to become angry"** (James 1:19). It seems even in biblical times, people loved the sound of their own voices.

Will we ever get back to days of more civil discourse? I pray we do. I believe that wise leaders and influencers can help change the tone of rhetoric in our nation. And those of us who profess Christ can especially lead the way as courteous listeners.

"Whoever has ears, let them hear" (Matthew 11:15).

Do for others
Katrina Harrmann

My dad used to play Yahtzee with me when I was a kid. There was something about that game that I just loved . . . rolling the five dice and hoping all the numbers turned up the same. I asked him to play with me, and he always did. He never rolled his eyes and sighed and never said he was too busy. He just put down whatever he was doing and sat at the old dining room table with me and played.

As an adult, I found out, to my surprise, that Yahtzee isn't my dad's favorite game. Not even close! Yet he played that silly game with me time after time, because he knew it brought me joy.

It's rare these days to find people doing things for others, isn't it? It doesn't happen a lot. People tend to do things for themselves—whatever makes them happy or requires the least effort.

This simple game of Yahtzee still reminds me that sometimes it's a great thing to set aside your own preferences and "do" for others. Do you want to spend an evening on the couch, but someone needs a home-cooked meal? Do you want to watch Netflix in peace, but your elderly neighbor is struggling to carry in their groceries or mow their lawn?

Following our heavenly Father's example and "doing" for others can be life-changing for those on the receiving and the giving end.

"Finally, all of you, be like-minded, be sympathetic, love one another, be compassionate and humble" (1 Peter 3:8).

Chasing faithfulness
Matt Ewart

If God's goal is for you to be with him forever in heaven, does it really matter how you live your life here on earth? Jesus taught that it does matter, but not for the reasons you might think. Here's an excerpt from one of his parables that talks about the importance of your life:

"The man who had received five bags of gold brought the other five. 'Master,' he said, 'you entrusted me with five bags of gold. See, I have gained five more.' His master replied, 'Well done, good and faithful servant!'" (Matthew 25:20,21).

The idea contained in this parable is not that you should spend your life chasing success. The king didn't say, "Well done, good and successful servant!"

He commended the servant's faithfulness, not his success. The servant did the best he could with what he was given, and that delighted the king.

It is so easy to get caught up in success, thinking every achievement proves you're a somebody.

It's also easy to get caught up in failure, thinking every mistake proves that you're a nobody.

For a moment, consider what it means that God's opinion of you has nothing to do with your successes or failures. He has already judged you in Christ. Your successes and failures went into his tomb, and something even better walked out three days later. You have life and hope.

So don't chase success. Don't let failure ruin you. Seek to be faithful with what God has entrusted to you.

I beg your pardon
Liz Schroeder

"Then Manoah prayed to the Lᴏʀᴅ: 'Pardon your servant, Lord. I beg you to let the man of God you sent to us come again to teach us how to bring up the boy who is to be born'" (Judges 13:8).

A little context: Manoah and his wife were unable to have kids. An angel of the Lord appeared to his wife and told her she would have a son (Samson). The angel also told her that Samson was supposed to follow a strict order of living where he would not drink any wine or eat anything unclean, among other restrictions. When Manoah's wife told him all that had happened, he wanted to get some clarification, so he prayed.

This all took place about three thousand years ago, but the time was not so different from now: "In those days Israel had no king; everyone did as they saw fit" (Judges 21:25).

In these days, everyone does as they see fit. If you are on the exciting roller coaster of parenting, Manoah's prayer is more than appropriate: "Lord, please teach me how to bring up this child!" Raising kids takes more wisdom, patience, and stamina than any human possesses. On top of that, if you are raising a child to follow Christ, you will face even more challenges. In these days, it seems like it is celebrated to let a kid be anything he or she wants to be—except a follower of Christ.

Parenting will bring you to your knees, so you might as well start there.

Jesus gets us
Clark Schultz

Batman has Robin. Shaggy has Scooby. Jordan had Pippen. A friend is one who gets you and your quirks, gets your odd sense of humor, and can relate to what you are going through. A good friend is the person who can sympathize and empathize with you.

The Dynamic Duo gets each other because they can relate to fighting crime. The Mystery Machine crew is always in search of a mystery while some are in search of the kitchen. And debate who's the GOAT in hoops if you want, but when the chips were down, one Bull picked the other up. Who does that for you?

Your heart was broken by an affair. Who is your hero to cry with? You're struggling with addiction. Who is the one who drives you to rehab? You just lowered a casket into the ground. Who is the friend who picks you up when all seems lost?

Having a true friend is wonderful, but remember that Jesus is your best Friend. He too felt pain; the nails of the cross pierced his flesh. Jesus was tempted by Satan like we are every day. Jesus felt the hurt of friends leaving him and ultimately the sting of death. He not only sympathizes with us, but his heart goes out to us because he truly gets us. He's not just a friend who says, "Man, this stinks. I wish I could know what you're going through." No, he's the only one who can, does, and delivers when he says, **"I will give you rest"** (Matthew 11:28).

Don't touch it
Clark Schultz

While on a six-hour car trip, this conversation actually took place:

Five-year old: "Mom, my lip hurts when I touch it."

Mom: "Well, then don't touch your lip."

Five-year-old: "Okay."

While it made a few miles of Chicago traffic humorous, it also made me think of a time that wasn't as lighthearted.

In the Garden of Eden, Eve was talking to the serpent. Bad idea.

Satan: **"Did God really say, 'You must not eat from any tree in the garden'?"**

Eve: **"God did say, 'You must not eat fruit from the tree that is in the middle of the garden, and you must not touch it'"** (Genesis 3:1,3).

Eve's answer to Satan is similar to the car-ride scenario: "Don't touch it." Her answer seems harmless and makes sense. But God hadn't said that. He had commanded Adam and Eve simply not to eat from the tree.

Was Eve trying to help God out or was it to help herself out of a temptation? Like Eve, we may feel we are helping God out by blurring the lines of right and wrong. We often change the pages of Scripture to fit our own agendas or lifestyles. Adding or subtracting to God's Word never ends well. What a blessing that Jesus came in human flesh to journey through life for you and me. What was undone by a tree in the garden was recovered by Jesus on a tree in the shape a cross.

Satan, you've lost!
Ann Jahns

What's your biggest fear? Mine is spiders. Despite what a wise kindergartner once told me—that spiders are "very useful animals"—I'm not having it. I've heard too many death-by-spider stories. Every morning as I peel back the shower curtain, I also keep my eyes peeled for any furry, furtive movement.

Here's a possible fear you might have—the devil. Yes?

Too many people don't believe in the devil. One of the biggest mistakes we can make is underestimating his power and his unrelenting desire to destroy our faith. That's exactly what he wants us to do. Jesus calls the devil **"a murderer from the beginning, not holding to the truth, for there is no truth in him. . . . He is a liar and the father of lies"** (John 8:44).

The devil knows how to exploit all our human frailties, leveraging everything from the tiniest lies he plants in our minds to full-blown, life-shattering temptations to try to separate us from God.

But 1 John 3:8 tells us plainly why Jesus came to earth: **"The reason the Son of God appeared was to destroy the devil's work."** And destroy it he did, in glorious, decisive fashion on Easter as he descended into hell to announce to Satan: "You've lost. They are mine! You will never take them away from me."

Should we be wary of the devil? Yes. But thanks to Jesus, we don't fear him.

Like fighting a toddler
Matt Ewart

Picture a toddler—a little boy just beyond the baby stage who is toddling around with chubby cheeks that jiggle with every step.

Now that I've gotten you to smile, imagine that this toddler is very angry at you with tantrum-level anger. He starts hitting you with his chubby little fists, pattering against your leg over and over.

Here's a silly question: How many times would he have to hit you for you to defend yourself and fight back?

Now that the smile has left your face, I'm hoping that your answer is the same as mine. You would never have to fight back. He's a toddler. If anything, you might restrain him so he doesn't hurt himself by trying to hurt you.

Chances are small (but not zero) that you'll be attacked by a toddler today. Chances are much higher that someone closer to your age will hurt you in some way. They might say something offensive. They might take something that's yours. They might humiliate you. Maybe it has already happened.

Because of what Jesus gave you, the threat level in these situations is similar to that of a toddler who's swinging his little fists at you. He can't hurt you. Nobody can devalue your self-worth that is tied to Christ. Nobody can dim Christ's light that shines through you. And nobody can rob the home that's awaiting you in heaven.

"Who shall separate us from the love of Christ?" (Romans 8:35).

Nobody. Especially not a toddler.

Direction, action, Person
Mike Novotny

Before words like *sanctification* or *discipleship* described the Christian life, "walking with God" was the Bible's preferred metaphor. **"Enoch walked faithfully with God"** (Genesis 5:22). **"Noah . . . walked faithfully with God"** (Genesis 6:9). **"The Lord appeared to [Abraham] and said, 'I am God Almighty; walk before me faithfully'"** (Genesis 17:1). **"And what does the Lord require of you? To act justly and to love mercy and to walk humbly with your God"** (Micah 6:8). When Jesus, who was God walking on our earth, wanted people to become believers, he most commonly invited, "Follow me," which is another way of saying, "Walk with God."

Why would walking be the number-one way to describe our spiritual lives? I can think of three reasons, which I'm excited to explain to you in the devotions to come. For now, here's a quick summary to get your gears turning: To walk with *God*, you have to be moving in God's direction. To *walk* with God, you have to be taking steps or personal action. To walk *with* God, you are blessed to be accompanied by a certain Person.

Read those last three sentences again. They matter more than almost anything else in your life. Direction, action, Person. That's what it means to walk with God.

Walking *with* God
Mike Novotny

This might seem insultingly obvious, but "walking *with* God" implies walking with God. It means choosing the path that God is on, joining him on the narrow and rarely traveled road of righteousness. In a world that runs after short-term pleasure, Jesus urges us to **"seek first"** the things that last forever by walking with God (Matthew 6:33). I won't lie. It's not the easiest direction to choose. But I can promise you that this direction leads to a glorious destination.

One summer my family hiked the Hidden Lake Trail at Glacier National Park. It wasn't an easy path, which climbed a few hundred feet over a couple of miles and was still snow-covered in certain spots despite being late June. But when we got to the end of the trail, none of us regretted the path we had chosen. Beautiful Bearhat Mountain towered above Hidden Lake with its deep glacial blue water. We were wowed and tried to capture God's glory with our man-made devices.

I imagine your Christian life, like mine, has not been easy all the time. Trusting God when you have cancer. Denying a desire within you. Loving someone who is nearly impossible to love. But please remember that the Christian direction leads to the best destination, a heaven that will make Hidden Lake look lame, a place that St. Paul called **"surpassingly great"** (2 Corinthians 12:7).

Keep walking *with* God. You are one day and one step closer to your glorious destination!

Take a step!
Mike Novotny

"Walking with God" implies *walking* with God. Seems obvious, right? It means moving when God is moving, taking action when God calls you to obedience. This is why Paul urges, **"Let us keep in step with the Spirit"** (Galatians 5:25).

I picture the Holy Spirit like my wife. Kim is a fast-walking woman who was raised by her mother, Candi, an equally fast-walking woman. You can only imagine what it is like to be my kids on a family vacation with their long-legged, marathon-runner dad and their on-the-move mom! We push them pretty hard so they can see more of the world than those who are sitting around.

God's Spirit pushes the pace too, and he wants you to keep in step. When temptation comes, he's moving fast into obedience, holiness, and trust. Can you picture him? When you're annoyed with someone, he immediately steps toward a deep breath, toward patience, toward not snapping in anger. When you are thinking about a past sin, he leaps toward grace, toward the cross, toward remembering the God who remembers your sins no more. He loves you too much to let you sit down in sin and shame. That's why he wants you to keep in step.

The next time you are tempted, picture the Spirit stepping ahead, looking back in love, and encouraging you to keep up. Then take a step! Because there's nothing better than *walking* with God.

With you every step of the way
Mike Novotny

This might seem as insultingly obvious as my last two devotions, but "walking with God" implies walking *with* God. It means that your entire life is not a lonely journey to God but instead is a lengthy journey *with* God. God is with you every step of the way to encourage you, listen to you, and carry you when necessary.

King David loved that aspect of his walk. In his most famous song, he wrote, **"Even though I walk through the darkest valley, I will fear no evil, for you are with me"** (Psalm 23:4). The road of life can take you through some pretty dark valleys, but you don't have to be afraid, because you are walking *with* God.

Are you grieving today? rubbing aching joints? praying for your headache to go away? stressed by family drama? frustrated by your continual struggle with sin or the lack of struggle by a loved one living in sin? Do you see no solution to the brokenness of our culture or of your own family tree? If so, don't be afraid. Your faith is not a walk to God. It's a walk *with God*. And your Father won't let you take a single step without being right by your side.

"Those who hope in the Lord will renew their strength. They will soar on wings like eagles; they will run and not grow weary, they will walk and not be faint" (Isaiah 40:31).

Carrying you home
Mike Novotny

I once planned a family hike to a beautiful waterfall in Yellowstone National Park, but before we got to the water, our youngest daughter hit a wall. We were miles from our destination when she ran out of gas, so I crouched down and said, "If you don't walk faster, a grizzly will get you."

Just kidding. I crouched down and invited, "Hop on." As I walked toward our destination with my beloved on my back, I could feel her joy increase. She was overwhelmed by a distance she didn't think she could walk, so the ride was a delightful surprise. When I finally set her down 1,554 steps later (we counted ☺), she was a different kid.

Jesus does something similar but so much better. He knows that heaven is equally beautiful and unreachable for our little human legs, which is why he carries us. Not for 1,554 steps or for a few miles but from start to finish. Peter wrote, **"Christ also suffered once for sins, the righteous for the unrighteous, to bring you to God"** (1 Peter 3:18).

There is such joy in those words! How do you get to God? By walking fast enough? By grinding out enough spiritual steps of obedience? No. Just Jesus. Jesus suffered to bring you to God. The cross carries you all the way to the Father's presence. Your "walk with God" is not an overwhelming, keep-up-or-a-grizzly-hell-awaits-you walk. No, it's a joyful journey with the God who will carry you home.

What a walk!

About the Writers

Pastor Mike Novotny pours his Jesus-based joy into his ministry as a pastor at The CORE (Appleton, Wisconsin) and as the lead speaker for Time of Grace, a global media ministry that connects people to God through television, print, and digital resources. Unafraid to bring grace and truth to the toughest topics of our time, he has written numerous books, including *3 Words That Will Change Your Life*, *What's Big Starts Small*, *When Life Hurts*, and *Taboo: Topics Christians Should Be Talking About but Don't*. Mike lives with his wife, Kim, and their two daughters, Brooklyn and Maya; runs long distances; and plays soccer with other middle-aged men whose best days are long behind them. To find more books by Pastor Mike, go to timeofgrace.store.

Linda Buxa is a freelance communications professional as well as a regular blogger and contributing writer for Time of Grace Ministry. Linda is the author of *Dig In! Family Devotions to Feed Your Faith*, *Parenting by Prayer*, *Made for Friendship*, *Visible Faith*, and *How to Fight Anxiety With Joy*. She and her husband, Greg, have lived in Alaska, Washington D.C., and California. After Greg retired from the military, they moved to Wisconsin, where they settled on 11.7 acres. Because their three children insisted on getting older, using their gifts, and pursuing goals, Greg and Linda recently entered the empty-nest stage of life. The sign in her kitchen sums up the past 24 years of marriage: "You call it chaos; we call it family."

Andrea Delwiche lives in Wisconsin with her husband, three kids, dog, cat, and a goldfish pond full of fish. She enjoys reading, knitting, and road-tripping with her family. Although a lifelong believer, she began to come into a deeper understanding of what it means to follow Christ far into adulthood (always a beginner on that journey!). Andrea has facilitated a Christian discussion group for women at her church for many years and recently published a book of poetry—*The Book of Burning Questions*.

Pastor Jon Enter served as a pastor in West Palm Beach, Florida, for ten years. He is now a campus pastor and instructor at St. Croix Lutheran Academy in St. Paul, Minnesota. Jon also serves as a regular speaker on Grace Talks video devotions and a contributing writer to the ministry. He once led a tour at his college, and the Lord had him meet his future wife, Debbi. They have four daughters: Violet, Lydia, Eden, and Maggie.

Pastor Matt Ewart and his wife, Amy, have been blessed with three children who keep life interesting. Matt is currently a pastor in Lakeville, Minnesota, and has previously served as a pastor in Colorado and Arizona.

Jan Gompper spent most of her career teaching theatre at Wisconsin Lutheran College in Milwaukee. She also served six years as a cohost for *Time of Grace* during its start-up years. She has collaborated on two faith-based musicals, numerous Christian songs, and has written and codirected scripts for a Christian video series. She and her husband now reside in the Tampa area, where she continues to practice her acting craft and coach aspiring acting students as opportunities arise. She also assists with Sunday school and other church-related activities.

Katrina Harrmann lives in southwest Michigan with her photographer husband, Nathan, and their three kids. A lifelong Christian, she attended journalism school at the

University of Missouri, Columbia, and worked at the *Green Bay Press-Gazette* and the *Sheboygan Press* before taking on the full-time job of motherhood. Currently, she is an editor for Whirlpool and lives along the shores of Lake Michigan and enjoys gardening, hiking, camping, doing puzzles, and playing with her chihuahua in her free time.

Ann Jahns and her husband live in Wisconsin as recent empty nesters, having had the joy of raising three boys to adulthood. She is a marketing coordinator for a Christian church body and a freelance proofreader and copy editor. Ann has been privileged to teach Sunday school and lead Bible studies for women of all ages. One of her passions is supporting women in the "sandwich generation" as they experience the unique joys and challenges of raising children while supporting aging parents.

Paul Mattek is a development director at Time of Grace. His great passions are design and Jesus, and as such his personal mission is to show people God's beauty in whatever way possible. He loves that at Time of Grace he gets to grow the ministry by meeting people and reminding them about the incredible love of Jesus—the best "sales" job ever. Paul and his wife, Julia, have four children—June, Louis, Elias, and Penelope (Penny)—and a pet guinea pig, Cinnamon.

Pastor Nathan Nass serves at Christ the King Lutheran Church in Tulsa, Oklahoma. Prior to moving to Oklahoma, he served at churches in Wisconsin, Minnesota, Texas, and Georgia. He and his wife, Emily, have four children. You can find more sermons and devotions on his blog: upsidedownsavior.home.blog.

Pastor Dave Scharf served as a pastor in Greenville, Wisconsin, and now serves as a professor of theology at Martin Luther College in Minnesota. He has presented at numerous leadership, outreach, and missionary conferences across the country. He is a contributing writer for Time of Grace and a speaker for Grace Talks video devotions. Dave and his wife have six children.

Liz Schroeder is a Resilient Recovery coach, a ministry that allows her to go into sober living homes and share the love and hope of Jesus with men and women recently out of rehab or prison. It has been a dream of hers to write Grace Moments, a resource she has used for years in homeschooling her five children. After going on a mission trip to Malawi through an organization called Kingdom Workers, she now serves on its U.S. board of directors. She and her husband, John, are privileged to live in Phoenix and call CrossWalk their church home.

Pastor Clark Schultz loves Jesus; his wife, Kristin, and their three boys; the Green Bay Packers; Milwaukee Brewers; Wisconsin Badgers; and—of course—Batman. His ministry stops are all in Wisconsin and include a vicar year in Green Bay, tutoring and recruiting for Christian ministry at a high school in Watertown, teacher/coach at a Christian high school in Lake Mills, and a pastor in Cedar Grove. He currently serves as a pastor in West Bend and is the author of the book *5-Minute Bible Studies: For Teens*. Pastor Clark's favorite quote is, "Find something you love to do and you will never work a day in your life."

About Time of Grace

Time of Grace is for people who are experiencing the highest of highs or have hit rock bottom or are anywhere in between. That's because through Time of Grace, you will be reminded that the One who can help you in your life, the God of forgiveness and grace and mercy, is not far away. He is right here with you. God is here! He will help you on your spiritual journey. Walk with us at timeofgrace.org.

To discover more, please visit **timeofgrace.org** or call **800.661.3311**.

Help share God's message of grace!

Every gift you give helps Time of Grace reach people around the world with the good news of Jesus. Your generosity and prayer support take the gospel of grace to others through our ministry outreach and help them experience a satisfied life as they see God all around them.

Give today at timeofgrace.org/give or by calling 800.661.3311.

Thank you!

TIME OF GRACE®